SMUDGED *by the* CINDERS

A JOURNEY OUT OF A LIFE OF LESS-THAN

KRISTIN-DANIELLE TALLEY

WESTBOW
PRESS
A DIVISION OF THOMAS NELSON

WestBow Press books may be ordered through booksellers or by contacting:

WestBow Press
A Division of Thomas Nelson
1663 Liberty Drive
Bloomington, IN 47403
www.westbowpress.com
1-(866) 928-1240

ISBN: 978-1-4497-4438-0 (sc)
ISBN: 978-1-4497-4437-3 (hc)
ISBN: 978-1-4497-4521-9 (e)

Library of Congress Control Number: 2012905448

Printed in the United States of America

WestBow Press rev. date: 04/16/2012

To my mother

Table of Contents

Introduction

"How lonely sits the city that was full of people! She has become like a widow who was once great among the nations! She who was a princess among the provinces has become a forced laborer!"—Lamentations 1:1

When I was a little girl, I wanted to be Cinderella. I dreamed and wished for a fairytale life. More than anything I desired to be the pretty princess with Prince Charming coming for me on his valiant white horse. As I've grown older that desire hasn't changed. Daily I seek for ways to think and feel like a princess. My prevailing need is still to have a courageous Prince charge over a hill, slaying dragons and evil magic just to find me . . . just to know my love.

I truly believe that within us all is the desire to be a princess. At some point in their lives, every little girl (even you tomboys), if only for a split second, dreams of what it would be like to be a princess. What would it be like to be Snow White brought back to life by true love's kiss? How exciting to be Rapunzel as an adoring prince scales the highest tower just to be in your presence? Better yet, how totally awesome would it be to wear those off-the-wall girly ball gowns, delicate slippers, and a smashing gold crown? How extravagant to be a beautiful princess forced into labor by your evil step-mother only to be restored to your position as princess by a Prince who moved heaven and earth to find you?

A princess is a woman or girl in a royal family, usually a daughter of a reigning king or queen. Princesses are typically thought of as beautiful, gracious, and sought after. When I speak of being a princess, these are the definitions I have in mind. I believe a true princess is compassionate, strong, bold, and courageous. Too often we are embarrassed to say we want to be princesses because over the years they have gotten a bad rap. They are thought of as wilting powerless things fretting in a corner somewhere but this is far from the truth! As we'll find out throughout this book, a princess of the One true King, God our Father, is anything but powerless and fearful. Her destiny to be rescued by the Prince, Jesus, does not detract from her own abilities or talents. You will find that to be wrapped up in the arms of Jesus releases us from the grip of our enemy, the Devil, and allows us to live freely as the strong, courageous women of God we are.

The desire to be a princess is a precious gift God has given to each one of us. It's a gift that gently nudges us towards and quietly reminds us of the destiny God has for His beloved daughters. It has always been God's design that we live as royalty. In his book, "Finding Favor with The King", Tommy Tenney questions, "Is it any accident that the dream of a 'Princess Bride' is so persistent even in contemporary societies, generations after true earthly royalty became rare? Could it be that our Creator planted this dream deep inside our hearts as a hidden seed, an eternal dream waiting to be fulfilled at just the right time?" I believe it is by divine design that we long for the fairytale existence. I believe the "Princess Bride" dream persists because it has been hard wired into our make-up by a loving Creator.

When we are younger, it is very easy to see ourselves as royalty. Our throne is just an imagination away. If asked we would state with regal authority that, "Yes we are Princess So-and-so and yes that is Prince Charming by our side." Unfortunately, somewhere between the little girl twirling with her pretend tiara and the young woman trying to feel comfortable in her own skin, we sometimes lose that certainty. While the desire to be a princess remains constant, the hope of actually becoming a princess gets tucked away with other childhood memories. Life happens. Hurt, pain, sin, and shame often happen. The princess within becomes alien and is replaced by what Lamentations calls a "forced laborer" or what I'd call a "cinder girl".

Lamentations begins with a broken Judah. Where once it was a bustling city full of people, it now lays empty, desolate, and forced into slavery by a foreign country. Jeremiah, the author of Lamentations, compares Judah to a princess dethroned who has become a forced laborer. At night, she weeps bitterly and her enemies have become her masters. The story sounds familiar, right? It sounds a lot like the story of a poor cinder girl named Ella.

Ella's story is that of a girl who lived the life of royalty only to have it tragically ripped away. She lived many years in solitude and forced labor. At this low point in her life it was very easy to forget who she was and from where she came. Her resting place was a bed of cinders; very soon she became smudged by those cinders and those cinders began to define her. This is what has happened to so many of us. We start off innocent and hopeful. I believe regardless of the home we grew up in, there is a time in our childhood where we all know what it means to be loved by the One True King. Then something happens; for some of us it happens very early in life and others may reach adolescence before it happens. This "something" changes the way we see ourselves and our King. Whatever this something is, it seems to snatch us from our thrones and thrust us waist deep in a bed of cinders. We then let these "cinders" define us or smudge our face. It becomes the part of ourselves we believe everyone around us can see. We begin to live a life of less than because of the shame that comes from these cinders smudging our face.

Within this book I pray you allow God to show you the journey out of the cinders and into your birthright as a Princess of the King of Kings. It is important to note that this is not a self-help book. There are no formulas as to how to make your cinders magically disappear. Within these pages is an invitation to know your Prince Jesus more intimately. Each chapter also ends with a prayer. It's important to pray The Word daily. When you pray the word you know you are praying The King's will for your life. I pray you will learn to trust Him as He guides you out of the cinders and into the realization of who you are in the Kingdom of God. It is my deepest prayer that in the end, you will find yourself no longer smudged by the cinders.

Ella and the Cinders

Once upon a time, Ella's life was filled with richness and beauty. She lived happily in a village ruled by a righteous and loving king who adored his people. Daily, he reminded them how precious they were to him. He especially loved Ella. When she was a small child, he found her wandering the streets of his kingdom, alone and afraid. He adopted her and made her his daughter. Every morning, he greeted her with a loving embrace. "My beautiful daughter, do you know how precious you are to me? Always remember you are my princess, and you are destined for greatness!" Tears would run down his cheeks as he thought of how much he loved Ella and the wonderful woman she would one day become.

Ella knew nothing but her father's love and joy. She spent her days by his side; where he went, Ella followed. Every night, before the last candle was blown out, Ella talked with her father about the adventures they'd had during the day. He always ended their days the same way they began; by reminding her how beautiful, precious, and loved she was. He told her about the prince and how she was destined to be his bride—it had been decided the moment the king found her. Ella would drift off to sleep with images of a beautiful castle, the prince, and her life with him dancing through her dreams.

But then, one day, Ella was spirited away from the castle in the night by a dark and evil force. Everything happened so quickly that she barely had a chance to process what had happened. Her world was turned upside down in a matter of days. Ella had been truly happy in her life with her father, the king. He'd loved her and taken every chance he could to tell her so. Now he was gone, and she would never hear his voice again.

She hoped it was all a dream—that at any moment she would wake up and her father would be smiling down at her, and she could rush into his arms for one of his special bear hugs. But as the carriage pulled up in front of a gray, oppressive, wooden cottage, she realized that it was no dream. Ella couldn't remember how she came to be in the carriage. She didn't know where she was or how to make her way back to her father's kingdom. Ella didn't even know who had taken her. All she knew was that she missed her father terribly and wondered if he was looking for her.

The Duchess met Ella at the door of the cottage, along with her two daughters, Delilah and Portia. The Duchess was the wicked owner of the gray cottage. She and her daughters regularly took in lost girls as their servants. Delilah and Portia stared piously down their noses at Ella, as The Duchess walked one full circle around her, scrutinizing every inch of her. "Not very pretty . . . actually somewhat plain."

"She looks more than a little weak, Mother," Delilah said.

"Can I have her clothes?" asked Portia.

"Of course, darling, she won't need them." With that, the duchess and her daughters spun on their heels and walked up the stairs.

A maid appeared out of nowhere and motioned for Ella to follow her. The maid led her farther and farther into the house, until they reached a large kitchen with no windows. "You sleep there," she growled, pointing to a small pallet of hay near the large fireplace at the rear of the room. A pillow, smudged by the flying cinders from the fireplace, was the only hint of comfort in the whole kitchen. Ella threw herself on the pallet and wept, unaware of the cinders falling on her tear-streaked face.

 CHAPTER 1 ⸻⸻⸻⸻⸻⸻⸻⸻⸻⸻⸻⸻⸻⸻⸻⸻

Into the Cinders

Cinderella is one of the most popular fairy tales ever told. I would be shocked to come across a female who hasn't heard or seen some version of this "rags to riches" story. It's been told and retold, made into a musical, and made into several bubblegum pop movies starring reigning "tween queens." What would possess me to retell it, let alone write an entire book based on this oft-told fairy tale?

I have to admit that as God placed this book in my heart, I asked the same question. I worried about being cliché. I tried to reduce it to a chapter in another not-so-cliché book but God kept leading me back to Ella, better known as Cinderella. The King of all Kings let me know there was a lesson to learn from the story of a poor little cinder-smudged kitchen maid named Ella.

The Definition of a Cinder

In our story, Ella has been taken away from her father. In the midst of her grief, she is carted off to a home where she must sleep and dwell in a place covered by cinders. Cinders are fragments of ash. They are the part of the ash that leaves soot marks on your face and hands if you get too close to a fire. Minor contact with cinders doesn't do much damage. It's annoying, but with a little scrubbing, cinders are fairly easy to wash away. However, constant contact leaves a residue on your skin, fragments in your hair, and the smell of ash on your clothes. From the moment she left her father's presence and entered The Duchess's home, Ella's face was smudged by those cinders—painful reminders of how far she had fallen.

Historically throughout the Bible, when tragedy struck someone, that person would rip their clothing and drown themself in ashes. It was a way to tell the world, "Hey! This situation hurts! I am mourning the good I have lost! See my shame!" Anyone who walked by this person knew something horrible had happened. The person's problems left a stubborn mark that was not easily washed away.

In Jeremiah 6:26, God says, "O my people, put on sackcloth and roll in ashes; mourn with bitter wailing as for an only son, for suddenly the destroyer will come upon us." At the time, Jeremiah was prophesying about the invasion of Jerusalem, and God was trying to impress on the people exactly how painful this time period would be. Later, during the Mede's takeover of Jerusalem, the prophet Daniel remembered Jeremiah's prophesy and "set [his] face toward the Lord God to make request by prayer and supplications, with fasting, sackcloth, and ashes" (Daniel 9:3 NKJV). Daniel was attempting to show God that he mourned what Jerusalem had lost—that they had found themselves separated from their heavenly Father, and it was painful. He confessed that they had sinned and done wrong. In each case the word translated as "ashes" is the Hebrew word *epher*, which is used figuratively to mean "worthless." During Jerusalem's time of intense pain, shame, and mourning, they covered themselves in ashes, representing their feelings of worthlessness.

If a cinder is a fragment of ash, then I suppose a good question would be what are ashes? One of the definitions of ash is *something that symbolizes grief, humiliation, or repentance.* Spiritually, cinders are the fragments of hurt, sin, and emotional sickness that cause grief or humiliation to smudge our lives—hopefully leading us toward repentance. Just as the invasion of their promised land made Jerusalem feel worthless at moments, our cinders often make us feel worthless. They are the lingering effects of negative life experiences that we have been unable to let go of. Prolonged exposure to them leaves a residue on our life, destiny, and ministry. When we trust in our own power, that residue cannot be washed away. It is our cinder smudges and trusting in our own power to wash them away that keeps us bound by them.

The Cinders that Bind Us

In meeting Christ, we have a sense of conviction about what we have done before, and it drives us to repentance. Cinders develop when that sense of conviction devolves into condemnation. Even when what has been done was done to us, we can still feel a sense of guilt and condemnation. We know God and we know he sent his Son Jesus to save us, but we can't seem to forget everything bad that has happened in our life. When we can't let go, we become bound by and smudged by the various cinders of life.

You will continuously come across two phrases in this book: "journey out of the cinders" and "wash away cinders." Our journey out of the cinders calls for us to deliberately change our behavior, our mindset, and the words we speak. To embark on the journey means we are making a conscious decision to no longer live a life less than the one God destined for us. The washing away of the cinders is left in the hands of our King and our Prince. We can journey out of the cinders, but it is the grace and mercy of God that will wash away the residual effects of our time in the cinders.

All of life's cinders can be split into four categories: public sin, private sin, emotional distress, and hurt. No matter what has happened or what you have done, those things that feel so overwhelming and unconquerable can fit into four tiny boxes and be overcome.

Later, we will talk about our journey out of the cinders. However, for the moment, it is important that you understand the various types of cinders and the affect they have on our relationship with the Prince.

Public Sins

The life we led before coming to Christ (and sometimes after coming to Christ) can be cringe-worthy. It's embarrassing to remember that we used to do anything we were big and bad enough to do. Some of us were drinkers, some abused drugs, some had sex outside of marriage, and some were blatant liars. The list can go on, and no matter where we land on the list, we wish it were all just a distant nightmare that never really happened. Unfortunately, those things *did* happen. Much of the time, the fact that some people in our lives remember those past sins is more troublesome than the physical consequence of the sin itself.

The cinders of Public Sin usually exist because no matter how you try to change, people remind you of where you came from and what you did. It's hard to understand how God could use you amongst the people who know what you have done. When God calls us, one of our first excuses for not heeding the call is, "God, people remember who I was and what I used to do. How can I minister to them? How can I prove to them I am a different person?" We become afraid that we will mess up again and then we beat ourselves up for not being perfect. It is these actions that allow the cinders of Public Sin to smudge our face.

I call this the "Moses Conundrum". In Exodus 3, Moses has the burning bush experience. God met him on a mountain, revealed Himself, and called Moses to deliver His people from the hands of the Egyptians. Instead of saying, "Sure, Great I Am, let's go," Moses began to think back over his past, where he'd come from, and doubts that he could accomplish the task began to seep in. His conversation with God went something like this:

"But why me, God?"

"Don't worry, Moses, I'll be with you."

"Uh huh . . . yeah . . . see, they may not trust me. You know who I am right? You know . . . I'm Moses . . . the stutterer. I'm not really good with words. You might want to send someone else."

"Your words will be my words. Don't fret."

"Hmmm. Okay, but remember I killed that Egyptian? That's why I ran out here to the desert in the first place."

This continued until finally, in anger, God said He would send Aaron as Moses' mouth piece. What I have always found funny is that a God that can set a bush aflame without singeing it probably knows who he is dealing with. God doesn't make mistakes and he never calls someone by accident. He knew Moses's past and he knows ours, yet he calls us still. Your testimony is what makes you perfect for what God has in store for you. He takes into account every piece of our history and of our character and sets a path designed specifically for us. No one has your experiences; therefore no one can accomplish your calling the way you would.

Moses thought of all of the bad he had done but he never thought how his unique experience could assist in the deliverance of God's people. He had lived among the highest class of Egyptians and yet was 100% Hebrew. That life experience would be useful when communicating with both the Israelites and the Egyptians, but Moses initially chose to allow the cinders of what he used to be define him, keeping him from following God's lead.

To begin living a life unhindered by the cinders of Public Sin, remember that these sins are nothing new to God. The fact that there are people who remember those things we used to do only makes our deliverance more miraculous. It further shows that God has a plan for everyone. Trusting in God's plan, humbly accepting that not everyone is going to believe you are changed, realizing it is not your job to convince them, and submitting your past to the tender mercies of God will allow the King of Kings to wash away the cinders of Public Sin.

Private Sins

I believe one of the reasons God wanted me to write this book besides the healing and deliverance of His many cinder smudged daughters is so that I could go through my own process of healing and deliverance. I have personally experienced each of the four cinder types and none was as insidious as the cinders of Private Sin.

Once upon a time I played the part of "Super Christian". On the outside I was the picture of someone totally sold out to Christ. I appeared to love praise and worship and I was very active in my local ministry. However, no one knew that I struggled with spirits of pornography and lust.

My introduction to pornographic material came at the age of five when a relative left a box of dirty magazines under the guest bed upstairs in our house. I don't remember why I was upstairs in the guest bedroom and I don't remember why I was looking under the bed (come on . . . I was five) but I remember with vivid clarity the images in those magazines. Throughout my life those images would haunt me only to be joined by new more graphic images as I entered adulthood. It became an addiction I hid away deep within my heart. On Sundays, as the praise team would go forth, all I could do was go through the motions, too ashamed to really offer any praise to God. As this secret weighed heavily on my heart, the very idea of church became oppressive and the idea of ministering to others filled me with resentment. When I looked in the mirror, all that could be seen was this very private hateful sin.

For many years I blamed that family member for my sin. If they hadn't brought the material into the house, I never would have been trapped. I blamed generational unclean spirits and anything else I could possibly think of to justify my inability to overcome pornography. On a superficial level my justifications were correct, maybe things would have turned out differently if that material wasn't under that bed and we know generational unclean spirits do exist. However, deep down, I knew that at some point I had to stop blaming others and seek God for deliverance for myself. I had to come to grips with my own actions and the things in my life that left me open to these unclean spirits.

Private Sins are disastrous because in them we lack accountability and usually continue in them without much resistance. Without accountability, it becomes simple to justify our actions to ourselves because no one knows what we are doing and therefore cannot assist us in combating the sins with the Word of God. Cinders of Private Sins are the easiest to cover up and the hardest to wash away. They are there smudging our face but we've become so adept at hiding the actual sin that hiding the cinder smudges feels like a walk in the park. Unlike all the other cinder types, those of private sin are rarely noticeable because we do a marvelous job of acting like everything is fine. Only we see the large marks spiritually streaking our face.

Cinders of Private Sins also distract us from who we really are because we cannot fathom anyone called by God could do the things we have done. It is hard to build a relationship with The Prince because we are terrified to approach Him. Approaching Him would mean confronting the private sins smudging our face. Most of us aren't sure we're ready to handle what God would have to say about these cinders. God can't wash them away because we are unable to admit to Him they exist.

Unlike cinders of public sin, the cinders of private sins are not only the residual effects of something done in the past but are present during the commission of the private sin. These sins are private because we understand that they are wrong and are ashamed to admit that we are struggling with a particular issue. Cinders are present when we are in the middle of self-condemnation and unable to accept Christ's mercy, grace, and forgiveness. This is the usual state of someone in the middle of private sins.

But I'm Naked . . . .

Genesis 3 describes what is known as the fall of man. Adam and Eve had given into their flesh and eaten from the forbidden tree. It was in that moment of disobedience they understood what shame was. They realized they were naked. When they heard God approaching, they hid so that He would not see their guilt and shame. When God called out to them and Adam responded that they hid because of their nakedness, God asked, "Who told you that you were naked? Have you eaten from the tree that I commanded you not to eat from?" It was never God's intent for us to know sin and shame. It wasn't until Adam and Eve chose to act contrary to God's will that they realized their naked state and then they hid. They no longer wanted to walk in the garden with their Father. How could He possibly still want to walk with them?

That's the trap most of us fall into. We sin, we hide. We figure our sins are too deep and dark for Him to work through us or save us. To justify our actions we often blame what we've done on various people/things, just as Adam blamed Eve and Eve blamed the Serpent. Private sins are usually not our fault in our own minds. At moments we even justify them by blaming God using the excuse, "Well, He made me this way." Private Sin cinders will continue to smudge our faces as long as we continue to hide from God and shift blame to justify our actions.

Emotional Distress

If you have ever seen "Forrest Gump", you probably remember the scene when little Jenny is running away from her abusive father and as she finds a place to hide she prays, "Dear God, make me a bird, so I can fly far, far, far away from here." It's a running gag between my mother and me that when one of us is annoying the other we say this line. However, I can remember times when I whispered this prayer in earnest, wondering if God was listening or if he even cared what was happening down here on earth.

David cried out a similar prayer in Psalm 55:1-8. "*Listen to my prayer, O God, do not ignore my plea; hear me and answer me. My thoughts trouble me and I am distraught at the voice of the enemy, at the stares of the wicked; for they bring down suffering upon me and revile me in their anger. My heart is in anguish within me; the terrors of death assail me. Fear and trembling have beset me; horror has overwhelmed me. I said, "Oh, that I had the wings of a dove! I would fly away and be at rest—I would flee far away and stay in the desert; "Selah" I would hurry to my place of shelter, far from the tempest and storm.*"

David emotionally pleads with God to not ignore his cries. Overcome and distraught about his current predicament, he wishes he could be a bird to fly to a place of rest far away from the storm that rages against him. Cinders of Emotional Distress show up as depression, anxiety, and despair. Bulimia, anorexia, drug abuse, substance abuse, promiscuity, and self-mutilation are only a few of the conditions with which someone smudged by the cinders of emotional distress deals. These conditions are brought on by the feeling that something about you or your life is not right.

While the other cinders all wreak havoc on your mind; depression and anxiety actually originate in your mind and can intensify the effect of all the other cinders that smudge your face. All your thoughts, dreams, and desires are filtered through these emotions. They trouble you and the enemy uses them to speak disturbing thoughts to you. They are capable of reducing you to a fearful, trembling, mess. Thoughts of death become prevalent. It's a desperate state to be in and becoming a bird to fly far, far away is an ever present dream. You never feel worthy and you dwell on what you "should" be. You lack joy and peace of mind/heart. How can Christ love an outcast like you (i.e. you don't talk right, you don't dress right, you're overweight/underweight, you're not smart)?

In verse 16, David states, "But I call to God, and the Lord saves me." In verses 1-8 David was distressed but by verse 16 he was sure by calling on the Lord he would be saved. What had changed? How had his circumstances changed from those beginning verses to the latter verse? The answer is nothing. Nothing in his life had changed. He was still hounded by his enemies, he was still being threatened with death, and I'm guessing a shelter from the spiritual storm swirling around him would be welcomed. Yet, he was still assured and comforted by the thought that his King would save him. David never shied away from worshiping God. David was a man after God's own heart because no matter the circumstance, he still found his Father in heaven worthy of all praise and worship. He had a deep relationship with Him and so when the spirits of depression and anxiety tried to attack him, he turned to the Father and prayed instead of giving them any power.

Joy and peace come when we are confident in the power of our King. The cinders of emotional distress smudge our face when we are unsure of His power in our life and we allow ourselves to see our problems as "too big" for God. We don't spend time with Him so there is no way for us to know who he really is and how he sees us. David knew the Lord is close to the brokenhearted and saves those who are crushed in spirit. (Psalm 34:18) However, he only knew this because he spent time with the King and the words of his God drowned out the voices of his enemy.

Hurt

2 Samuel 13 tells the tragic story of a girl named Tamar. Tamar was one of the daughters of King David. She is described as beautiful and a virgin [pure and unspotted]. In fact she had a special garment that could only be worn by virgin daughters of the king. Tamar was so wonderful, Amnon, one of King David's sons, fell madly in "love" with her. Amnon became so frustrated about not being able to have Tamar as his own that he made himself sick. When the King came to visit his ill son, Amnon requested that Tamar come prepare a meal for him while he was on his sick bed.

Tamar trustingly arrives to do what was asked of her. Tamar had no reason to distrust her brother's motives. She remained with him even after he sent all the servants from the room because she trusted him, no matter how odd his actions appeared. Imagine her horror when her blood relative attacks her, trying to force her into bed with him. Think about the shame creeping into her mind as her begging and pleading falls on deaf ears. In the end Amnon is successful in raping his sister Tamar. Then, according to verse 15, "Amnon hated her exceedingly." After brutally attacking Tamar, his "love" was gone and Amnon no longer wanted her in his presence. He sent for a servant to remove her and bolt the door behind her! Violated, brutalized, and now rejected, verse 19 says, "Tamar put *ashes* on her head and tore the ornamented robe. She put her hand on her head and went away, weeping aloud as she went." Tamar lived out the rest of her days as what the Bible called a *desolate* woman.

Hurt and pain is inevitable in life. Oh, princesses, how I wish it weren't! For Tamar, her hurt came from someone she trusted and loved. Because of Amnon's cruelty Tamar became smudged by the cinders of hurt brought on by rape and incest. She never recovered and remained desolate. For some of you, Tamar's cinders are your cinders. Someone has done the unthinkable to you. For others someone's hurtful words bruised you. Unfortunately that someone is possibly a person you loved and trusted. Whether physical or emotional, their sin against you seems carved into your mind, reminding you someone didn't love you enough to maintain your innocence, purity, and everything that made you feel beautiful.

The trouble with the cinders of hurt is we feel justified in letting them smudge our face. "Let everyone see how they hurt me! Let everyone know my shame!" they yell out. We tear off our royal robes, robes that signify us as pure daughters of the King, and wallow in the cinders. You may not want the world to know exactly how you were hurt but you need someone . . . anyone . . . to know you are in pain. So you continue to wallow in the ashes. Even while seeking someone to know your pain, you isolate yourself because who can you trust really? Your heart becomes cold and bitter until it is hard to trust even Christ to really be there for you when you need him. The dictionary defines desolate as "devoid of visitors, joyless, showing the effects of abandonment and neglect; devoid of warmth, comfort, or hope." And that is what some become, a desolate woman.

While it seems impossible, the cinders of hurt will continue to smudge our face until we let go and forgive. We'll talk more about forgiveness later, however know this; dwelling on the hurt and associated anger only affects you. Most of the time those who hurt us have moved on while we stay tied up in knots. God wants to wash away the hurt and the cinders of Hurt from our lives but cannot as long as we hold onto them with a death grip. Princesses, let go.

Go And Sin No More

John 8:1-11 holds a familiar event. The Pharisees bring a young woman to the temple where Jesus is teaching, make her stand in front of everyone, and proclaims she is an adulteress. From the oldest to the youngest they are ready to stone her for this sin. Jesus, unconcerned with these men's motives, responded, "If any one of you is without sin, let him be the first to throw a stone at her." One by one all the men left until there was only the woman and Jesus.

All who had accused her could not condemn her because they had also sinned at one point or another. In the end, Jesus didn't condemn her either. Instead he said to her, "Go and leave your life of sin." Two very important things happened in this story; 1) man wanted to condemn her, reminding everyone exactly who she was, and 2) Jesus didn't condemn her, choosing not to see her as man did, and responded, " . . . leave your *life* of sin."

Condemnation of Man

The constant in all the cinder types is "man". Man will wish to remind us of who we once were. Man will want to condemn us for our imperfections and at times will cause some of the issues with which we struggle. In order to prepare ourselves for this journey out of the cinders, we must understand that no one is perfect. Throughout this book, anytime you feel overwhelmed by the opinion of people, remember, "No one is perfect." We often spend so much time worrying about what people think, say, and feel about who we are that we block out the fact that everyone has skeletons. Romans 3:23 says, "For all have sinned and fallen short of the glory of God." (NKJV) When you find yourselves caught up in the approval of man, remember that every person you come across has at one time found themselves outside the Father's will and because we are flawed human beings they will most likely find themselves there again.

Being a follower of Christ and being cinder free is not about having it all together. It isn't about being perfect. Perfection isn't something to which any of us should attain. Being a true Christian and living a life free of cinder smudges lies in this truth, "For God so loved the world, he gave his only begotten Son, that no man should perish but have everlasting life." (John 3:16 NKJV) The King of kings looked down on his creation, understood that we would make mistakes, and sent his Son to die so that we can be free from those mistakes.

My Pastor recently preached a message titled, "Never Give Up". In his message he stated that there are three opinions in life that matter; 1) God's opinion of you, 2) Your opinion of God, and 3) Your opinion of yourself. God sees you as His Beloved Princess. He sees you as someone He loved so much that he would sacrifice His Son. In return He asks only that you realize He is sovereign King over all. There is nothing too big for Him to handle, including our cinders. When we understand the first two points, it becomes easier to see ourselves as the princesses we are and dismiss the negative words of the world.

Leave Your Life of Sin

What I find interesting about Jesus' words is the understanding behind them. He didn't say go and never sin again. He said, "Leave your life of sin." Jesus understood that there is a difference between sinning and living a life of sin. The most devout Christian will sin. As we become more mature in Christ, the frequency of our sins should drastically decrease but we are human and we will sin. This doesn't mean we are no longer children of the King. It does mean that, when we do slip, we make our way to the throne of grace asking forgiveness.

When one leads a life of sin, it is a conscious and deliberate decision to disobey the will of God without thought of repentance. A life of sin is devoid of the redemptive powers of Christ. There is stubbornness to our actions when we lead a life encompassed by sin. When Jesus told the adulteress to leave her life of sin, he wasn't stating she would never sin again but that she should leave behind her the behavior that was moving her farther away from God.

No Condemnation

Whether we are struggling with cinders of public sin, private sin, emotional distress, or hurt, if we ever want to be free from them the first step is to recognize that there is therefore now no condemnation to those who are in Christ Jesus, who do not walk according to the flesh, but according to the Spirit. (Romans 8:1 NKJV) When we begin to hold this truth in our heart we can begin to let The Prince wash the cinders from our face. Cinder smudges only exist because of our own self-condemnation; they have nothing to do with Christ's feelings or thoughts towards us. As we go through this journey out of the cinders, it is important to always remember that we have been forgiven of our sins and that our hurt and shame were taken to the cross by our Prince Jesus.

Pray The Word:

Father,

I acknowledge I have fed on ashes up until now instead of feasting on and remembering your Word. Due to this my heart has been deceived by the enemy and I've allowed it to mislead me. I admit I have a hard time recognizing if the things I am holding on to for security are lies. Yet you still call me to remember that you made me, I am yours, and I am not forgotten. You see my cinders and you have swept them away like a cloud. My sins and my hurt are like the morning mist. I return to you and you wash away the cinders of my past.
(Isaiah 44:20-22)

In the Name of Prince Jesus I Pray,

Amen

CHAPTER 2

A Cindered Existence

I believe the story of Cinder Ella has survived so long because we can relate to her plight. She was the beloved daughter of her father when tragedy struck and left her alone in a bed of cinders. The cinders smudged her hands and face. She was forced to labor for a wicked woman and the princess within became a distant memory. She felt unworthy of Prince Charming as she was and could not see a way out of her current predicament.

A cinder girl is essentially this; a beloved daughter of the King of all kings who finds themselves living a cindered existence (a life of less than) with no foreseeable escape or rescue. She is usually plagued by feelings of inadequacy, shame, and guilt. Due to this, they feel unworthy of the love of the true Prince, Jesus Christ. Her focus is often on what she has lost and the hole that is left behind. Her thoughts are continually turned inward towards self instead of out towards her King and her Prince. Day after day she dwells on the absence of her Father.

O God, Be Not Still

I want to make an oddly obvious statement; to have a journey out of or escape the cinders means that at some point we had to journey into the cinders. Duh, right? Many people feel as if one day they wake up and their whole life has crumbled beneath them. However there was a series of events that had to occur before the world crumbling. Ella's journey to a cindered existence seems to begin with the sudden absence of her father. Where was he? Why hadn't he stopped the person who had taken her away from Him?

The same could be said for us. Our journey seems to begin with the absence of God our Father. In Psalm 83:1, David prays, "O God, do not keep silent; be not quiet, O God, be not still." I can almost imagine him alone in his room feeling a deep longing for his heavenly Father who has become dishearteningly silent. The worst feeling in existence is found in the times when our precious Father seems absent and silent. Where is God and how could He leave us to wallow in our cinders?

Deuteronomy 31 begins with Moses announcement that Joshua would succeed him as leader of Israel. He begins to encourage them, reminding the people of their covenant with God, and ensuring them that any nation or obstacle that comes their way can be overcome. In verse 6, he encourages them to, "Be strong and courageous. Do not be afraid or terrified because of them, for the Lord your God goes with you; he will never leave you nor forsake you." This was so important for the people of Israel to understand that Moses repeated again in verse 8, "The Lord himself goes before you and will be with you; he will never leave you nor forsake you. Do not be afraid; do not be discouraged."

Princess of the One True King, we can claim this promise as well. Our Father goes before us and has promised to never leave us or forsake us. God never leaves us. God never disappears. He is never absent from our lives. Then the question remains, if our Father never leaves us, how can our journey into the cinders begin with His disappearance? It doesn't. Ella's journey truly started the moment someone or something plotted to change her life and our journey begins with whatever moves between us and the presence of God.

God is always with us, his presence never leaves us, but sometimes things happen within us that begin to shut God out making him feel very far away or even totally absent. Most often it is our own inability to come to him, whether it's because we are too ashamed of our sins, we are too hurt by man, or because we've allowed the voice of enemy to be louder than the voice of our King. It is the cinders of life that distracts us and distances us from our Father and they didn't happen suddenly. Usually it happens gradually and almost unnoticeable to an unfocused mind. It isn't until we look around and begin to notice the effects of long term cinder contact that we realize we have been living a cindered life.

A life of "less than" was never The Father's plan for his royal daughters. From the very beginning he desired for us to live an abundant life filled with knowledge of His love and acceptance. He never wanted us to be in bondage to our pasts and our mistakes. He sent his son, The Prince Jesus, to die on the cross just so we could be delivered from bondage and live our lives out as Princesses. However, the moment sin happens, hurt happens, or we become overwhelmed by the circumstances of life, without an understanding of our worth to The King, we begin to live a cindered lifestyle. Any one smudged by the cinders, living a cindered existence, is plagued by a lack of self-worth, a lack of purpose and destiny, as well as a lack of peace.

Lack of Self-Worth

Those of us who have been in church most of our life have heard more times than we can count that we are children of The King. We hear it in Sunday school, Bible study, Sunday morning worship, and every other time we walk through the church doors. It has become a Christian catch phrase. "Hallelujah! I'm a child of The King." Yet, I wonder how many people say it just to say and how many say it because they believe it?

When you are a child of a king, you are heir to his throne. A king is sovereign which means they have complete control of their universe. If you are a child of the king, whatever he controls you also control. A child of a king commands respect, honor, and power where ever they go within their father's kingdom. They walk with authority and the expectation that they will be treated as royalty. Think of Paris Hilton. She isn't someone I would consider to be a role model and I often disagree with her behavior but as heiress to the Hilton fortune, she expects that whatever she wants she will get. The idea that she is unworthy of inheriting the Hilton dynasty has never crossed her mind. She knows her lineage and walks in the authority the Hilton name gives her.

Our Father is the King of the entire universe. There is nothing outside of his control. As children of the King we should command the respect, honor, and power that accompany the title "Princess of the One True King". There isn't a man on Earth or a demon in Hell that shouldn't bow to our dominion and authority. There is a quote that I read recently that has stayed with me; "I'm the type of woman that when I wake up, the devil says, 'Darn, she's up again.'" Only a woman who knows her worth and understands her position in the kingdom of God can upset Satan just by waking up.

When we lack self-worth or don't understand how much we are truly worth, we will continue to live in the cinders. You can easily spot a princess who doesn't understand her full worth; her walk lacks confidence, she has a hard time meeting someone's eyes, and she is constantly adjusting her attire, her hair, or anything in an attempt to make herself feel presentable.

On our journey out of the cinders, it is important to understand who we are and what we are worth. Our worth is determined by our Father in heaven and he finds us so precious that he sent His son to redeem us on the cross. I have to repeat John 3:16. "For God so loved the world that he gave his one and only Son, that whoever believes in him shall not perish but have eternal life." (NIV) I realize that scripture may seem overused at first, however, think carefully about what it means. Can you think of anyone else in your life that would give the life of their child so that you may live? You are worth Jesus sacrificing himself on the cross for your sins.

Lack of Purpose and Destiny

There is a reason we are all here. Not one person on Earth was born by accident. Jeremiah 29:11 says, "'For I know the plans I have for you,' declares the Lord, 'plans to prosper you and not to harm you, plans to give you hope and a future.'" (NIV) Quite often when we are smudged by the cinders of life, it is hard to see any future worth mentioning. It feels like the cinders are where we will dwell for the rest of our life. What frequently happens is we walk through life aimlessly with no real plan or destination; we're just serving time until we can get to heaven. This is not the life our King had planned for us. His plans are to prosper us, give hope, and a future. He wants our life on earth to be fulfilling and fruitful. He isn't looking for our time here to be waiting station.

Our cinders block this plan from our view. They make us fearful to step out on faith and pursue our King given dreams because we aren't certain we really deserve them. It is safer to believe we aren't meant for anything special because there is no risk involved. A cindered existence conditions us to believe we are meant to be average but a Princess free from cinders understands we are all meant to lead extraordinary lives full of God's purpose and destiny.

Lack of a Sense of Peace

In the world, when nations are at peace, it means there are no wars or confrontations to deal with. When we are at peace, there is a lack of turmoil and contention within us. When one is at peace, they are calm; they feel a sense of comfort and contentment. However, when living a cindered existence, peace is hard to find. Everything about our life seems tumultuous, chaotic, stormy, and without comfort. When there is no peace in your life, even a restful night's sleep would appear to be out of the realm of possibility.

Peace is found in Christ alone. Those separated from The Prince by their cinders will never know the comfort and peace that radiates from him. However, when we realize He isn't looking for perfection and draw closer to him, then we experience what David sings in Psalm 29:11; "The Lord gives strength to his people; the Lord blesses his people with peace." Peace comes as we draw closer to our Prince. You will hear this maybe a hundred more times throughout this book. Draw closer to The Prince, cinders and all. Draw ever closer. Find worth, purpose, and peace within His embrace.

In order to be free from a cindered existence, we have to build intimacy with The Prince, allow Him to wash away our cinders, and rest in His unconditional love. We cannot wait until we have washed away our own cinders because we don't have the power to do so. Right now, determine within your heart to draw closer to our Prince.

Pray Today:

Father,

You have commanded me to be strong and courageous even in the times when I don't feel your presence. I don't have to be terrified or discouraged because you have promised to be with me wherever I go. (Joshua 1:9) I know you have plans for me. They are plans to prosper me and not to harm me. It is these plans that give me a future and give me hope. (Jeremiah 29:11) Help me to remember that I am your daughter and that I am not destined to live a cinder smudged life; I am a Princess destined for a throne in your kingdom. I am led into your courts with joy and gladness. (Psalm 45:15)

In the Name of Prince Jesus I Pray,

Amen

Becoming Cinder Ella

Ella spent her mornings being pulled in different directions. Delilah wanted this to eat but Portia wanted that to eat. For Portia, the house was too cold but Delilah whined about the suffocating heat. In between their impossible demands each found time to taunt Ella. One particular morning, the sisters were unrelentingly cruel.

"Be careful not to touch any of my things Ella. I wouldn't want my clothes covered in your filthy cinders," Portia remarked from her perch on top of three dozen silken pillows.

"Oh, she can't help being dirty," Delilah chimed in, "What would you expect from a simple kitchen maid?"

"The least she could do is clean her face!"

"Why bother, it's just going to become all . . . cindery again. Isn't that right Cinder Ella?"

"Ooooh! I like that, Delilah," Portia cackled, "Cinder Ella! That is a perfect name for her! And all our Cinder Ella is ever going to be is a dirty, filthy, orphaned kitchen maid sleeping in a hearth full of ashes." The sisters began to laugh uncontrollably as Ella hurried away.

Outside their room, she crashed suddenly into the maid. Bedding and toiletries flew everywhere. Ella mumbled an apology and tried to help the maid pick up a capsized pile of towels. As she absent mindedly picked up another silk sheet from the floor, she realized the maid was saying something to her.

"You shouldn't let them bother you so much."

"What's that," Ella said, finally paying attention.

"You can't help your face being smudge by the cinders. It's the life you were supposed to lead, so why let them bring you down about something you have no control over."

"No," Ella whispered, "This is not the life I was supposed to lead. I'm supposed to be a princess in the courts of The Prince. My father told me so."

"I'm just trying to prepare you. I've been here a long time. My father told me I was a princess too and then I ended up here. I've learned the longer you hold on to that princess fantasy, the harder it will be here for you. You are a cinder girl, Cinder Ella. If you accept that it will be much easier for you." With that, the maid picked up the last towel and walked away.

Ella ran to a mirror that was right outside of the sisters' bedroom door and stared tearfully at her reflection. She yanked a rag from her apron pocket and began to rub furiously at every dark smudge on her face. She glared again at her reflection, but it was no different. Finding a vase filled with water on a nearby table she dipped the rag into it. Ella scrubbed her face with the wet cold rag to no avail. Another quick glance in the mirror revealed that not one mark was gone . . . not one smudge had disappeared! The sisters are right. The maid is right. I will never be anymore than Cinder Ella. Years will go by and I will still be sleeping in that little straw bed by the hearth covered in cinders!

Chapter 3

Cinder Stokers

Samuel 1:1-8 introduces us to Peninnah and Hannah. Both women were married to Elkanah son of Jeroham. Peninnah had managed to give Elkanah many children, however Hannah had not. Verses 5-7 tell us that Elkanah loved Hannah tremendously but the Lord had closed her womb and because of this her rival Peninnah would provoke her to bitter tears. In those days, a woman who was unable to bear children for her husband was considered "less than" and in some cases the people believed it was because the woman had sinned that she was unable to have children. Hannah may have felt unworthy of and maybe even disbelieved the love Elkanah freely gave her and often asked God why he wouldn't open her womb. She looked at Peninnah, who seemed to have it all, and felt "less than".

Peninnah, however, knew the truth. She had all the worldly goods but Hannah had Elkanah's love. Hannah had favor with Elkanah. How this must have rubbed at Peninnah's last nerve! She had provided her husband many sons and daughters but still he loved Hannah more. Peninnah played on Hannah's insecurities mercilessly. 1Samuel 1:6 says that Peninnah "kept provoking [Hannah] in order to irritate her." Why? It wasn't just out of jealousy but also because she didn't want Hannah to realize how special she really was to Elkanah.

Cinder Stokers Defined

Peninnah is the definition of a "Cinder Stoker". To stoke means to increase the activity, intensity, or amount of something. Cinder Stokers do just that; they increase the activity, intensity, or amount of cinders in our lives. The Cinder Stokers of the world continuously and in some instances almost joyously remind us of our past hurt and shame. They seem to have the uncanny ability to hone in on our deepest darkest insecurities, magnify them, and then use them against us.

Cinder Stokers often appear to possess everything you want and need (they wouldn't be effective if they didn't!), however ask yourself this question; if they really had it going on, why do they waste their time on you? Why spend their energy trying to convince a little cinder girl that a cinder girl is all she'll ever be. The answer is they don't have it all. Something is missing deep inside and it tears them apart. Even while you are smudged by the cinders, they recognize the fact that you have the potential to come out of your situation and that bothers them because they don't see a way out of theirs. Keeping you in your place makes them feel better about theirs.

The Words of a Cinder Stoker

Job understands what it means to live a cindered existence. He also understands the concept of Cinder Stokers. In Job 1, we find him happy, rich, and faithfully serving God. Then by no fault of his, Job finds it all taken away. He spent his days covered in ashes, picking at festering sores, and wondering what happened to his life. Enters the first Cinder Stoker . . . *his own wife!* Even through his difficult situation, Job had held on to his faith in God's sovereignty. His wife, however, did not. She looked at their current predicament and could not understand why God had treated them so poorly and it ate at her that Job did not feel the same way. Finally she says to him, "Are you still holding on to your integrity? Curse God and die!"

Cinder Stokers must be a curious bunch because their words are frequently peppered with questions. "Why are you doing it that way?" "How do you keep going?" "Don't you think that dress is a little short?" "Have you stopped dieting?" "I wonder why God would let this happen to you?" They aren't actually interested in your life. These questions are to cause you to doubt who you are and who God is. Can you imagine being Job, already downtrodden, feeling somewhat defeated, and then your wife comes to you and says, "Are you nuts? Just give up!" Can you imagine how he felt? Job responded to her with continued trust in God but I can see where it could have caused someone to stop for a moment and think, "Why don't I just give up?"

Asking seemingly harmless questions are an easy way to begin to manipulate or control someone who isn't grounded in the words of our King. It is also one of the easiest ways to plant seeds of doubt. If a cinder stoker can get someone to begin questioning themselves, it isn't long before the cinder girl begins to believe whatever negative thoughts a cinder stoker has introduced into their mind. The words of a cinder stoker will first cause doubt in our situation, then they will cause us to question ourselves, and finally we begin to question God's plans and feelings toward us. Once that happens, it is easy to keep us in a cindered existence.

The Heart of a Cinder Stoker

Cinder Stokers are the bully you dealt with in high school. They are the relative who picked at you during family dinners. They can be the boss who berates you in front of other co-workers. Cinder Stokers are the significant other/husband that physically abuses you or family friend that molested you. The point is that Cinder Stokers show up in a variety of ways but their purpose is always the same; to keep you in bondage to the devil and under their thumb.

It is an issue of control and status. Cinder Stokers attack in order to be in control over someone because they often feel a lack of control in their own life. They attempt to keep a cinder girl in the ashes and smudged by the cinders because their own insecurities dictate the only way they can feel good about themselves is if they make someone "better" than them feel little and small. They feel that there is something magnificently unique and different about the cinder girl and they can't find that quality in themselves. They cannot stand for others to be more "beautiful" because of their own ugly hearts.

Girls Will Be Girls

Maggie opened her locker and immediately every book fell to floor at her feet. Laughter and snickers met her ears as she scrambled to pick up the contents of her disheveled locker. "What is she wearing?" she heard from behind her. Maggie glanced down at her clothes. She was wearing the brand new shirt and jeans her Mom had bought her last week. When she'd looked in the mirror that morning, for once she'd felt beautiful. "I know, how she even squeezed herself into that is beyond me," someone else responded. Maggie felt tears gather in her eyes, grabbed her jacket, and pulled it on as she hurried to put the last of her stuff in her locker. The bell rang and she rushed to class.

"You're late, Maggie," Mr. Andersen huffed, glancing at the clock.

"Sorry," she barely mumbled.

"Well, take your seat," he barked.

Laughter again followed her to her seat. Maggie slid as low as possible in her chair and began counting the moments until last bell. She said a silent prayer to be invisible, however almost immediately she began to feel tiny paper wads being flicked at her desk. Maggie hurried from class the moment the bell rang and hid in the last stall of the girls' restrooms.

She heaved from desperate sobs wondering why she hadn't noticed the clothes she wore made her look heavier. She wondered why she couldn't be like the other girls. Her thoughts drifted to why she had to be so different. Her final reflection before she fell asleep huddled between the toilet and the cold stall wall was why God had seen it necessary to make someone like her. How could she be useful to Him?

The name may be different but the story is familiar to many of us. How often in our adolescence and sometimes in adulthood did we encounter the one person who made us feel smaller than small? I added this story because too frequently we discount the bullying we experienced during our younger years. Teachers, parents, and friends made light of the situation by promoting the "kids will be kids" brand of conflict resolution, but how many of us remember the first time a group of kids snickered our way and even now it gives us pause?

I remember my freshman year of high school plaid pleated skirts were really popular. The first day of school I wore one of maybe six plaid skirts my mother had just purchased for me. I felt invincible and smoking hot . . . until I stepped off the bus. Immediately a group of guys began to giggle and one shouted, "Look how big her legs are!" Already struggling with my weight, that comment crushed my fourteen years old heart. I went through the school day tugging at my hemline praying it would miraculously grow longer. I never wore another one of those skirts. Sadly I was in my twenties before I even considered wearing a pair of *shorts* in public again.

We often like to think it doesn't, but the negative words spoken to us when we are younger affect the people we are today. They shape our insecurities and often our view of who we are physically. As we journey out of the cinders, it is important to look back on these incidents, deal honestly with how they affected us, and then submit the incident to God in prayer. Why? When we start getting rid of deep seated insecurities that have followed us from puberty, we give less fodder to Cinder Stokers. They can't use what no longer exists. If we give our issues about our body image, our intellect, and our purpose to our King of kings then Cinder

Stokers can't use them to increase the intensity of the cinders smudging our face.

It is important to recognize the true identity of Cinder Stokers; they are sad imperfect people in need of our forgiveness and prayer. If we view them realistically instead of glamourizing them, it will be easier to diminish the affect they have on our lives. We often view Cinder Stokers as better than us for whatever reason; maybe we believe they are prettier than us or smarter than us but remember Our King created each and every one of us in his image. He made us unique for a reason. When the words and actions of Cinder Stokers threaten to make you doubt your royal status pray to God our Father to allow you to see yourself the way he sees you.

Pray Today:

Father,

I thank you for you have set me apart for yourself and you hear me when I call to you. (Psalm 4:3) I lay before you all my cares and insecurities because I know you care for me. (1 Peter 5:7) I praise you because I am wonderfully and fearfully made. (Psalm 139:14) I trust more in your words than I do the words of my Cinder Stokers. I will not say to them, "I will pay you back for this wrong," but I will wait on you to handle each situation. (Proverbs 20:22) I will live in harmony with the Cinder Stokers of the world. I will be sympathetic, loving, compassionate, and humble. I will not repay evil with evil or insult with insult but instead with blessing because I know you called me to this so that I may also be blessed. (1 Peter 3:8-9) Bless them and heal their hearts so they may find the joy and peace I am discovering within you every day.

In the Name of Prince Jesus I Pray,

Amen

 CHAPTER 4 ————————————————————————————

Cinder Dwellers

We all know that one person who, no matter what, is in the midst of a perpetual pity party. Even when they are giving a good report, their words are still gloom and doom. If they are sick, it's to death. If they are healthy, it's about time for that winter flu. Their outlook is pessimistic at best. They are what I call Cinder Dwellers.

Cinder Dwellers are those who find themselves living a cindered existence, make no effort to rise from the cinders, and will attempt to keep others in the cinders as well. Cinder Dwellers usually aren't malicious in their actions. Somewhere along the line they stopped believing in deliverance or abundant life and their goal is to save other cinder girls pain by acquainting them with "real life".

I'm Just Trying to Prepare You!

My mother recently convinced me to join her on a Women's Prayer Retreat somewhere out in the middle of nowhere. Approximately forty women trudged out to one of Michigan's freezing lakes to seek God's face. While I was apprehensive about just how close I could get to God while suffering from hypothermia I went anyway. The weekend was marked by tremendous breakthroughs and the tangible palpable presence of God. It was impossible to feel anything but excitement and extreme faith in God's divine plan for His children. The last day of the retreat, all on a spiritual high, several young women and I sat down to breakfast. As always with young single women the conversation eventually turned excitedly to our future husbands.

"God is really working on me and preparing me," exclaimed one girl.

"I know," another chimed in, "I've already prayed about the type of man I want and I believe God will send Him. He's just preparing us a little more."

No one had noticed the older married woman sitting at the end of the table. The chatter continued, each of us telling our own tales of waiting for our Father chosen husband as the older woman looked back and forth at each glowing tender face. Finally, as if she could barely contain herself, she decided it was time to impart her matronly wisdom.

"Are you ready to take care of your husband and bath him if he gets sick days after you get married?"

Stunned silence fell over our table as we each searched for an appropriate response. Where had that question come from? The older woman continued, "If you're not ready to do that, if you're not ready to clean up his messes, then you are not ready to be married."

After a moment, one of the other young women answered carefully, "I believe that if that is the destiny God has for me and my husband, then He will prepare me somehow."

"Marriage isn't roses," the mature woman leveled, "And it's never what you think. You can pray about what you want but it doesn't turn out that way. I'm just trying to prepare you."

It was about that point in the conversation that I excused myself from the table. In my own journey out of the cinders, I've learned the tell-tale signs of a cinder dweller. I have found to argue with or entertain the thoughts of a cinder dweller is both fruitless and potentially detrimental to your personal journey out of the cinders. It may seem callous, however, remember the definition of a dweller is someone who is unwilling to rise from the cinders and will attempt to keep others there as well. While showing them love is a must, remaining separate from them is a necessity. You can love someone without allowing them to negatively influence your life.

The Words of a Cinder Dweller

The older woman wasn't trying to be mean. In her heart of hearts she truly believed she was trying to help. As in the case with most cinder dwellers, her life had probably been filled with disappointments for which she wished someone had prepared her. At first listen a cinder dwellers message may even seem correct, but a closer look will show their words don't line up with the word of God. In this case, the older woman had discounted the fact God desires the best for His children, answers their fervent prayers, and if storms are to come, he never leaves us unprepared. Psalms 37:4 and 5 says, "Delight thyself also in the Lord and he shall give thee the desires of thine heart. Commit thy way unto the Lord; trust also in him; and he shall bring it to pass."

Cinder Dwellers readily give advice in an effort to temper the "realities of life" for Cinder Girls. Their speech is peppered with phrase like, "I've been through what you've been through", "I'm just being real with you", and "I just want to prepare you". The phrases usually preclude what I call reverse motivation. "I've been through what you've been through and you'll never get over it, just pray for strength to endure", "I'm just being real with you; you can't succeed at that. Pray God shows you a more suitable dream", and my favorite, "I'm just preparing you for the worst".

You may look at these statements and think, "Who would ever listen to this nonsense?" You would be surprised what we believe as truth when in the midst of our cinders. In our weakened state, it is easy to allow these words to penetrate our heart. Satan uses them to pick at pre-existing doubt and insecurities. If we are not careful, we will begin to rehearse the words of the cinder dwellers and eventually become cinder dwellers ourselves.

The Heart of a Cinder Dweller

A cinder dweller's heart has been broken, usually more than once, by either the consequences of her private/public sins or the effects of hurt and emotional distress. Life dealt her a bum hand, leaving her feeling slighted and unprepared. She views those who have reclaimed their Princess status as naïve and prays it won't be too hard when the other shoe drops for them. She keeps her expectations low and her doubt high. Her faith is limited because for her to truly have faith in God's plan for her life she would have to let go of everything she has believed was truth.

The heart of a cinder dweller is turned inward towards self instead of outward towards God. She feels selfless but in all actuality is one of the most selfish people that exist. Continuing to dwell on her sins, her problems, her disappointments, and her shame makes it all about her. Her heart is filled with envy and jealousy. She has seen God do miraculous things for others and can't understand why not her. Unfortunately, it is her lack of faith, her selfishness, and her envy that keeps the Kings blessings from flowing in her life.

When it comes down to it, cinder dwellers are more focused on self than on God. They get caught up in self-condemnation, self-pity, and self-help. They can't always articulate it, but intuitively they know there is some disconnect between themselves and God and they blame themselves. All conversations, situations, and experiences are filtered through their jaded sense of self. Read the following passage from Romans 8:7-10, 14, and 15:

7 Focusing on the self is the opposite of focusing on God. Anyone completely absorbed in self ignores God, ends up thinking more about self than God. That person ignores who God is and what he is doing.

8 And God isn't pleased at being ignored.

9 But if God himself has taken up residence in your life, you can hardly be thinking more of yourself than of him. Anyone, of course, who has not welcomed this invisible but clearly present God, the Spirit of Christ, won't know what we're talking about.

10 But for you who welcome him, in whom he dwells—even though you still experience all the limitations of sin—you yourself experience life on God's terms.

14 God's Spirit beckons. There are things to do and places to go!

15 This resurrection life you received from God is not a timid, grave-tending life. It's adventurously expectant, greeting God with a childlike "What's next, Papa?" (MSG)

Cinder dwellers wind up ignoring God the Father and who He is because they are so focused on themselves. God regularly feels absent to them and they often question Him as to why. Notice what verse 9 says; "But if God himself has taken up residence in your life, you can hardly be thinking more of yourself than of him." Cinder dwellers know of God and if asked, I would venture a guess that they would say they had an intimate relationship with him, however it is impossible to be intimate with the Father and ignore him at the same time. They haven't truly welcomed him in; when those of us who have journeyed out of the cinders or those of us who have begun our journey begin to talk about the wonderful freeness we're experiencing, a cinder dweller won't be able to comprehend what we are talking about.

For those who welcome Him, allowing him to dwell within them instead of focusing on dwelling in the cinders, they will find themselves living on the Father's terms. His spirit calls out to their spirit daily, whispering to them their purpose and destiny. With an existence free of cinders, life becomes an adventure. I love the way verse 15 sums everything up. Unlike the cinder dweller, women free of cinders do not dread the unexpected events of the day or even the trials that will most assuredly come, because in the end they are living life on God's terms. For those who refuse to be cinder dwellers, each day they wake up with an excited, "What's next, Papa?"

Pray Today:

Father,

I thank you for the adventure you've laid before me. Reveal to me the cinder dwellers in my life. Help me to filter out the negativity of their words and attitudes. Show me any cinder dweller like tendencies in my own life. I want to live a life centered on you. I want to live a life focused on you. I want to experience life on your terms. When I wake up each morning, let the words, "What's next, Papa?" be on my lips. (Romans 8:7-10, 14-15)

In The Name of Prince Jesus,

Amen

CHAPTER 5

A Spiritual Enemy

One of the better action movies to be produced in the last couple of decades or so is Independence Day (ID4). ID4 has it all, explosions, an extraterrestrial fighting Will Smith, a battle that spans both Earth and the Cosmos, and finally an almost enigmatic foe. July 2nd, without warning, the world wakes up to find spaceships thought to be 9 miles wide hovering over their homes. No one knew where they came from, when they'd come, or what they planned to do. When the new visitors suddenly attack, decimating most of the world's major cities, there is wide spread panic as people agonize over the next step. Was it all a mistake? Could they mount a proper counter attack before the aliens destroy everything? Lead by the President of the United States the human race tries everything they possibly can to fight the enemy to no avail. They can't bypass the alien shields, the enemy has cut off their communication, and they lose more resources every time they move against the aliens. It looks hopeless. It is not until it is discovered that Earth has encountered these alien's before and that the alien technology is stored in a hidden US military base that our heroes find a glimmer of hope. They began to understand who their enemy was, where they came from, their purpose, and their strategies. The enemy was no longer unknown.

An Identifiable Enemy

If I were to ask you, who is your vilest enemy, would you say it's the girl at who used to pick on you in school? Is it the family member that hurt you so long ago? Could it be the cinder stokers or dwellers in your life? Very rarely would someone reply, "Satan." God has given man the gift of free will. We are responsible for our own actions. However, behind every attack of man is an enemy that would love nothing better than to see us draw away from God. Satan uses our human "enemies" to drive a wedge between us and our Prince.

It is impossible to fight an enemy we know nothing about. Anyone in the military would tell you that more important than the quantity of their artillery is the quality of their intelligence of the enemy. You can have all of the fire power in the world but if you don't have an idea regarding the purpose, strategies, and tactics of your opponent, victory is almost impossible. The same is true in the spiritual realm. We can have all the spiritual power on both heaven and earth but if we are ignorant to our enemy's motives and strategies we will be watching for the enemy to attack from the left when his plan is to overcome us from the right.

1 Peter 5:8 says, "Be self-controlled and alert. Your enemy the devil prowls around like a roaring lion looking for someone to devour." The enemy wants us discouraged and distracted by Dwellers and Stokers because if we're focused on them we can't be "sober and vigilant" and are easily devoured. I recently looked up how real lions catch and attack their prey. I found that lions aren't known for their stamina so they have to be close to their prey, therefore, they 1) typically target prey not close to the herd, distressed prey, at times prey already dead, 2) need some type of cover so their approach isn't seen, and 3) cannot manage prolonged attacks where they have to chase down prey.

These characteristics are the same for an attack by Satan. He targets those who have distanced themselves from other people of God and those that are distracted by distressing issues in their lives. If he attacks us outright, we'd see him coming and prepare ourselves so he uses subtlety and deception as cover. Finally, he can not manage prolonged attacks where he must chase us down. Don't get me wrong, he can last many rounds and even if he tires out he usually comes back harder than before, however he can not sustain a prolonged battle against a well prepared child of God.

Distanced

Ella was so easily overtaken by The Duchess and The Sisters because she was removed from her support system. The first thing Cinder Girls tend to do when they journey into a cindered existence is distance themselves from the people of God. Church becomes a hassle and any excuse not to go is welcomed. When smudged by the cinders, regular communion with believers feels awkward and at times offensive. Not wanting to leave herself vulnerable to any hurt or criticism, the Cinder Girl further isolates herself from the people of God, but believes it is they who have distanced themselves from her. Any slight offense or perceived offense becomes another reason not to gather together with the saints. In my own journey out of the cinders, distancing myself from other children of the King became a major issue. It was gradual. I missed a Sunday here and then another there. Then I dropped out of any ministry of which I was a member. That was pretty much the nail in the coffin. Even the most devout saint can not maintain regular attendance to church if they are not involved in a ministry.

It became a trust issue for me. While I was the one distancing myself, I blamed my church family for not chasing after me. I no longer trusted them to be there for me or to have my back if I needed them. There were definite issues that I had within my church and not all of the offenses were imagined, however I expected them to be super human and was unforgiving of their flaws. This is an easy way for a Cinder Girl to remove herself from fellowship with her church family. We will set unrealistic expectations for them to meet and when they inevitably fall short of those expectations we feel justified in isolating ourselves. However, the major flaw in this behavior is that we are placing all of our hope and trust in man instead of our King.

Every now and then, I find myself needing to work on trusting the church in which God has planted me; but more than trusting them, I daily have to learn to put my trust in God and honor Him by regularly making my way to His house. It is when we gather together that we can rest in the love of our brothers and sisters in Christ, build our arsenal to fight against the enemy through the hearing of the Word of God, and take courage from the testimonies from other former Cinder Girls. I think it is important to add that while sometimes it is necessary to leave a church, we need to prayerfully approach this decision. Sometimes we leave a church because of some offense when it is actually God's desire that we remain there because as a whole, the ministry is a church founded on the Word of God. Never leave angry, never leave hurt, and never leave before you clearly hear God directing you to go.

The entire purpose of our journey out of the cinders is to draw closer to our Prince. Jesus made it clear in Matthew 18:20 that, "For where two or three have gathered together in My name, I am there in their midst." (KJV) When we gather together with other believers, Jesus promises to be in the midst of that meeting. Our goal is to always be near the presence of the Prince and one of the ways to do this is to maintain regular attendance to church, Sunday school, or small group meetings.

Distracted

Once we've distanced ourselves, it becomes easy to get distracted. A distraction is anything that turns our focus and our attention away from a set goal or destination. In this case our destination is a life free of cinders and our goal is to reclaim our rightful places as princesses in the Kingdom of God. Hebrews 12:1-3 says it perfectly, "Do you see what this means—all those pioneers who blazed the way, all these veterans cheering us on? It means we better get on with it. Strip down, start running—and never quit! No extra spiritual fat, no parasitic sins. Keep your eyes on Jesus, who both began and finished this race we're in. Study how he did it. Because he never lost sight of where he was headed—that exhilarating finish in and with God—he could put up with anything along the way: Cross, shame, whatever. And now he's there, in the place of honor, right alongside God." (MSG)

Think carefully about what is distracting you from being the princess you are meant to be. Distractions aren't always as obvious as we think. Hebrews 12:1-3 doesn't only mention sin as a detour to our journey out of the cinders. It also talks about "extra spiritual fat". This pertains to those things that are not necessarily a sin but they aren't helpful to our journey either. Sometimes it's the music to which we listen. When we feed our spirit a steady diet of secular music, the messages within that music begins to take up residence in our heart. It becomes a distraction because quite often the spirit behind certain songs conflicts with the words of our Father the King. This can be true of movies, television, books, boyfriends, and best friends. Be conscious of those things that draw you away from The Prince and remove those distractions immediately. Unfortunately, the process of removing distractions can be a painful process. Anytime you remove something that has become a part of your life, there is a sense of loss followed by a period of mourning. However, as we begin to replace these distractions with the things of God, we soon find a joy and peace that makes the momentary discomfort worth it all. Always keep in mind 1 Corinthians 6:12, "All things are lawful unto me but not all things are expedient; all things are lawful for me but I will not be brought under the power of any." (KJV)

Chased Down by The Enemy

If you've ever participated in a sport, you are well aware that to compete successfully you need strength, endurance, and stamina. You can be strong but if you don't have endurance you won't push on when the competition gets rough. You can have endurance but if you don't have the stamina, you won't have the energy to continue. The same holds true when you find yourself being chased down by the enemy. When being chased by the enemy, the goal is not for us to flee from him but to make the devil flee from us; without strength, endurance, and stamina you have an almost nonexistent chance of succeeding.

Ephesians 6:12 reminds us, "For our struggle is not against flesh and blood, but against rulers, against the authorities, against the powers of this dark world and against the spiritual forces of evil in the heavenly realm." (NIV) The Message Bible translates Ephesians 6:12 this way, "This is no afternoon athletic contest that we'll walk away from and forget in a couple of hours. This is for keeps, a life-or-death fight to the finish against the Devil and all his angels." We aren't just fighting to live a cinder free life; we are fighting for our lives. If our true enemy is a spiritual enemy, then we need to learn to fight him in the spiritual realm. We gain our strength, endurance, and stamina not by physical calisthenics or weight lifting. We train using prayer, praise and worship, and fasting. (2 Corinthians 10:4)

Prayer

Think of prayer as our muscle. It is through prayer that we communicate with our Father and it is through prayer that we instigate change in the spirit realm. We need prayer to bind the works of the enemy and to loose blessings from heaven. (Matthew 18:18) During his time on Earth, Jesus regularly drew away from the crowds to pray and gather strength for what was to come. Before he was arrested, in Mark

14:34, Jesus told Peter, James, and John, "My soul is overwhelmed with sorrow to the point of death." Then he told them to stay and keep watch while he went farther ahead to pray. His impending death on the cross was weighing heavily on his soul and he needed to talk to his Father in Heaven to continue with his mission. In verse 36 he prayed, "Abba, Father, everything is possible for you. Take this cup from me. Yet not what I will, but what you will."

Jesus's flesh would desire Jesus to skip the cross entirely. Yet his spirit desired to do the will of God. If Jesus hadn't spent time with God daily praying to him, being comforted and encouraged by him, and being guided by his Father I don't believe he would have made it to the cross. We wouldn't have received salvation. That may seem odd to say at first; Jesus is the Son of God, sovereign, and holy. However, Jesus came to earth as a flesh and blood human being and was confronted by the same temptations as those he came to save. (Hebrews 4:15) He understood that to defeat Satan, he would need to use the same spiritual weapons he had taught his disciples. If the Son of God needed to use prayer to gain strength to combat the enemy then how much more do we mere mortals need to pray. (Mark 9:29)

In prayer, God will begin to guide and direct us. Through prayer, we will begin to bind the enemy instead of allowing the enemy to keep us in bondage to our cindered existence. When we pray to our King, we are both acknowledging who he is in our life and showing our love by drawing near to him. Psalm 91:14-16 says:

14 "Because he loves me," says the Lord, "I will rescue him; I will protect him, for he acknowledges my name.

15 He *will call upon me*, and I *will answer him*; I will be with him in trouble, I will deliver him and honor him.

16 With long life will I satisfy him and show him my salvation." (NIV, emphasis mine)

He has promised in his word that because we love him and acknowledge him, he will rescue us, protect us, and when we call on him he will answer us. He will protect us from the plans of Satan. He will be our strength.

Praise and Worship

A few years back, I was chaperoning our youth ministry's Spiritual Encounter. Once again I found myself out in the woods to commune with God, nature, and mosquitoes the size of baby pterodactyls. For three days we encouraged our teens to do everything possible to have an encounter with God. On our second day, we took them to an obstacle course that was about 40 feet high at its tallest point. The only way down was to complete one of several slightly terrifying obstacles.

Confession number one; I wasn't in the best physical shape. Working out and I had become enemies long before that moment so when I made it to the top of the obstacle course, the young guy at the top pointed me toward the easiest obstacle. When I started to move towards what was possibly the hardest course to traverse, he politely said, "That one is really difficult. It takes a lot of upper arm strength." That was the wrong thing for him to say. Confession number two; I am *super* competitive and can be prideful to a fault. I glanced at my flabby upper arms then back at the young man and without hesitation began across the ridiculously hard obstacle.

Midway through, bruises lining my arms and hands, I became increasingly aware that just maybe I should have listened to the kid. I was out of breath, my arms burned, my legs felt numb, and the end of the obstacle still felt miles away. I looked back at the kid and read all over his face, "I'm going to have to go out there and get the big chick." For a moment I felt like yelling, "Yes, I am out of shape, this was a bad decision, now come and get me." However, that would have meant admitting defeat. I hate losing, especially if winning or losing is within my control. I decided to endure. I stopped thinking about how my body felt, how impossible the situation seemed, how crazy the decision to keep going was, and just thought about the next inch I had to travel. When I made it through that inch, I focused on the next inch. On and on, inch by inch I moved forward with everything inside of me screaming stop. However, the reward of completing the most difficult obstacle course out there was too sweet; I could taste it. I finished after what seemed forever and all weekend long I wore my bruises like a badge of honor. I had been able to endure because instead of focusing on my physical limitations I focused on something outside of myself.

Praise and worship is not about us; it has nothing to do with our current situation, how we feel at the moment, or who is watching. Praise and worship does one thing; it points to the truth of who God is and that he is worthy of homage regardless of what is happening in our lives. He is sovereign, timeless, gracious, righteous, and just even if he decides today to stop blessing his children. God's character is not dependant on us. He is God all by himself. He is truly holy or by definition truly set-apart. By giving him praise and worship in any circumstance, we are recognizing his set-apartness, we are moving outside of ourselves, and we are moving to a place where all that matters is our King. Praise and worship is where our endurance comes from because it has nothing to do with us, it forces us to move outside of self and focus on God.

When we praise, we are offering grateful homage to our King. We are saying we are thankful for who he is and celebrating his character. Our praise declares his name to others. (Psalm 22:22) Praise is us telling Satan no matter what he brings against us; we still acknowledge God and his wonderfulness. It says we know the truth and that is what we choose to focus on.

Worship is when we humble ourselves and makes God the object of our reverence. Worship is his children giving to him the glory due his name. (Psalm 29:2) Whether it is through song, service, or material sacrifice, worshipping is saying, "I would give all I have to honor you, Father." What is important about praise and worship is that neither of these actions brings attention to the work of the enemy. It moves us to a place where we are intently focused on the works of Jesus and the character of God. This gives us the ability to combat the enemy with patient endurance.

Fasting

If you've ever played on an organized sports team and "forgotten" to train during the off season, you know that when the first practice of the season rolls around you'll be huffing and puffing more than the Big Bad Wolf. Your body is no longer conditioned to the rigors of game play. You don't have the same stamina you did when you ended last season. Stamina comes from keeping your body physically fit and conditioned. In order to be fit and conditioned in the spiritual realm, we need to fast.

Fasting encourages discipline and obedience. It helps us to receive revelation from God because fasting heightens our sensitivity to the Spirit of God. In Acts 13:2, there was a group of teachers and prophets at the church in Antioch, and "While they were worshiping the Lord and fasting, the Holy Spirit said, 'Set apart for me Barnabas and Saul for the work to which I have called them.'" The group was able to hear from the Holy Spirit because 1) their focus was on God through worship and 2) they were hungrier for the revelation of God than they were for food as evidenced by their fasting.

True fasting isn't about dieting. It isn't about giving up television or the internet (While for some of us giving up these items are truly a sacrifice, technically it wouldn't be considered fasting.) True fasting is about giving up food and on occasion drinks for a time in order to come to a place where we are hungry for God and earthly food is secondary. It is truly embracing, "Man does not live by bread alone but on every word that comes from the mouth of the Lord." (Deut. 8:3, NIV)

As I write this chapter, my church is currently going through our new year 21 day fast. As a body we are consecrating ourselves and seeking God's face for guidance, healing, and miracles throughout the next 12 months. I've never been the greatest "faster". Previously I have lacked the discipline to complete a one day fast let alone a 21 day fast. This year I purposed in my heart that I wanted more of God than I did of food. The first few days were difficult (there was a run in with a mushroom swiss burger that almost proved too tempting) but after about the third day, I hit this groove where I didn't really notice what I was giving up but instead I noticed what I was gaining. I have heard more from God in these days of fasting than I have ever before. While fasting, some of these chapters wrote themselves. I was amazed at how much God wanted to say to his cinder smudged princesses.

What has been a true blessing during this fast is that because I am conditioning my spirit and exercising my spirit, the enemy has been unsuccessful in trying to deter me from the purpose God has put in front of me. Satan has tried to discourage me and cause doubt but has been a dismal failure. I praise God for the joy and peace that comes through fasting. Fasting increases my faith as I listen to what the Lord has to say to me. I can say with confidence that if you want to stop the enemy in his tracks, build your strength through prayer, receive endurance through praise and worship, and increase your stamina through fasting.

Pray Today:

Father,

I thank you for your protection. The enemy would like to see me remain smudged by the cinders of my past. He has tried to distract me from my goals and distance me from the people of God. There are cinders in my life that I can only be delivered from through prayer and fasting. (Mark 9:29) Why should I be distanced or distracted by the enemy? Why should I be worried or anxious? I will praise and worship you, keeping my focus on your power. (Psalm 42:5) Help me build strength, endurance, and stamina through prayer, praise and worship, and fasting.

In the Name of Prince Jesus I Pray,

Amen

The Messenger Arrives

Early the next morning, a royal messenger arrived at the Duchess's door. Ella, having heard his horse approach, quickly answered the door so that Duchess and The Sisters would not be disturbed. The Royal Messenger handed her a delicate piece of parchment with gold leaf letters scrawled across the front.

"What is it?" she whispered.

"It's an invitation from The Prince. Tomorrow night he is holding a ball at his palace. Everyone is invited."

"Everyone?"

"Everyone," The Royal Messenger smiled and winked at her, "That includes you too Ella."

In awe, Ella began to shut the door and then something occurred to her. She spun back around to where The Messenger had just been standing. "How did you know my name?" But The Royal Messenger was gone! Ella glanced curiously at the invitation. It felt charged with possibilities. The Messenger had said everyone was invited. Not just the dukes, duchesses, lords, and ladies. Everyone was invited and that included her! She had a chance to meet The Prince. She would get to dance in his famous ballroom. Ella imagined herself in a wondrous gown, floating gracefully across the dance floor as The Prince asked her to dance. How spectacular!

"I suppose I can't expect a simple kitchen maid to know better than to stand around like an imbecile with the front door wide open admitting all types of insects," the Duchess's harsh voice came from behind her. Quicker than lightening, Duchess was upon her snatching the invitation from Ella's right hand, narrowly missing the left as she slammed the door. Ella scurried out of The Duchess's reach.

"What is this," the Duchess barked, impatiently waving the invitation.

"The Royal Messenger brought it. It's an invitation," Ella sputtered.

Immediately the Duchess's eyes lit up as she examined the parchment more intently. Ella watched frozen in her spot as the Duchess read the invitation three then four more times. The Duchess walked the full length of the hallway and back again, all the while smiling and muttering to herself. After a moment, the Duchess approached Ella.

"What do you think?"

"Think about what, Duchess?"

"The invitation," the Duchess snapped.

"Well, I think it would be lovely to go," Ella mumbled.

"Yes, quite. I assume you would like to go?"

"Can I?" Ella asked excitedly, forgetting to whom she was speaking.

"Of course not! Why on earth would The Prince want a dirty little wretch like you traipsing through his palace?"

"But it says everyone is invited."

"Everyone but you," The Duchess laughed.

"But The Messenger said . . ."

"I don't care what The Messenger said. You are not going. You are not worthy of attending such a fine occasion. Furthermore, you will be too busy preparing Portia and Delilah for the ball." The Duchess sauntered back up the stairs leaving a broken Ella behind her.

CHAPTER 6

An Invitation To Dance

High School can be brutal. It's not bad enough that you're at that age where your emotions and body spaz out on you but you have to deal with classes, unforgiving teachers, and the unrelenting social hierarchies that are "cliques". However, none of these things are more brutal than . . . the school dance. Dances were the bane of my existence when I was in school. Spending weeks wondering if I'd be asked to the dance and if I'm asked will it be by the guy I wanted to ask me. It was all exhausting. Then there was the crushing blow of not being asked at all. Rough stuff. Yet, those exhilarating moments where the guy of your teenage dreams asked you to homecoming (prom, etc.) would probably make the rejections worth it.

When Jesus asks us to dance, it's even more brilliant than any time a guy asks us to dance.

The Messenger

John 16:13 says, "But when he, the Spirit of truth, comes, he will guide you into all truth. He will not speak on his own; he will speak only what he hears, and he will tell you what is yet to come." (NLT) It is the work of the Holy Spirit that invites us to draw closer to our Prince. It is through the Holy Spirit that we receive understanding of God's will, God's desire for his children, and revelation when reading The Word of

God. He reveals what is in our Father inner thoughts as well as reminds us of the teachings of Jesus. The Holy Spirit is truly The Messenger.

It was the Holy Spirit that led Jesus into the wilderness to fast. Before Jesus ascended to Heaven after the resurrection, he instructed his followers to wait for the Holy Spirit before embarking on their mission's journeys. It is through the Holy Spirit our King gives us guidance. To sustain a life free of cinders, we must be in tune with the Spirit of God. We must be familiar with him and the power that comes from him. Embracing the Holy Spirit and realizing he is one of three facets of our King is a necessity. It is God's Holy Spirit within us that gives us the power, in the name of Jesus our Prince, to cause the devil to flee.

The Invitation

The bible declares, "Everything that goes into a life of pleasing God has been miraculously given to us by getting to know, personally and intimately, the One who invited us to God. The best invitation we ever received!" (2 Peter 1:3 MSG) The average persons comfort zone is 18 inches in radius meaning that when someone comes closer than 18 inches to your body, typically you will become uncomfortable if you don't have a close relationship with that person. When you dance with someone, you have to allow them into your personal comfort bubble. There has to be a certain amount of trust that the person will not abuse the privilege of entering that personal bubble. When Christ invites us to "dance", he is asking us to draw closer to Him, getting to know Him personally and intimately as the One who is inviting us into The Kingdom. He is asking us to 1) trust Him not to abuse the privilege of entering the deepest parts of our heart and 2) understand He trusts us with His inner thoughts and desires.

The fact that it is an invitation means we can accept or reject it. When we accept this invitation, everything that goes into a life of pleasing God is miraculously given to us. When we accept the invitation, everything we need to know about walking in God's will is implanted within us. The desire to wash away our own cinders disappears as we twirl with the Prince, allowing Him to accept us as is, therefore washing away the cinders that smudge us.

And She Dances

There is group at my church called the "God Chasers". They are a group of banner wavers/ dancers that minister during praise and worship on Sundays. I can't explain how beautiful it is to be singing praise to my King as the God Chasers dance and wave there banners in celebration. As a whole, the group regularly brings tears to my eyes. However, there is one woman who touches my heart. When praise and worship begins she starts to whirl and twirl with reckless abandon. Her whole demeanor changes; her focus seems to be firmly locked on enjoying this chance to dance before her Savior. You can tell that it's not about her but about Jesus. I look at her and I can almost see Jesus dancing with her. At times I am almost a little envious because I have yet moved to a place where I could dance that passionately in praise privately, let alone in public.

King David had that reckless abandon behavior when it came to dancing before his God. 2 Samuel 6:13,14 says that as David and the House of Israel were bringing the Ark of the Lord into the city, David danced with all his might; just being that near to the presence of God made David want to celebrate. The closer he came to God the more he danced and the less he thought about how others saw him. As David danced in the presence of God, when we accept Jesus' invitation, it will bring us closer to the true Prince and the closer we are to Him the more our spirits dance without regard to what people think about us.

What could move someone to such reckless abandon? The goal of Christ's invitation to dance is to bring us to a place where He can wipe the cinder smudges from our face. According to Psalm 30:11, "He turns wailing into dancing, removes our sackcloth, and clothes us in joy." Once we accept His invitation, He turns our current state into something beautiful. It is this something beautiful that prompts crazy, fevered, consuming praise.

An Invitation Lost

Ella had the invitation to the ball in her hand. She was that close and in a moment of decreased vigilance, The Duchess was able to snatch it away. Ella was left groveling to her enemy for permission to go to the ball and meet The Prince. Quite often, this is our plight. The Holy Spirit delivers the invitation to draw closer to The Prince to our hearts and because we are distracted, Satan is able to snatch the invitation away.

In Luke 8, Jesus tells the parable of "The Sower and The Seeds". He speaks of a sower who went out to plant some seeds. Some of the seeds fell by the wayside, were trampled, and devoured by the birds of the air. Jesus explained later that the seed was the word of God and that, "Those by the wayside are the ones who hear; then the devil comes and takes away the word out of their hearts, lest they should believe and be saved." (Luke 8:12) The invitation to dance is brought by The Messenger through the Word of God. The Prince's desire to have an intimate relationship with us is clearly laid out within the bible. This invitation is meant to stay in our heart and provoke us to believe in our Prince, however, when we aren't focused, the enemy is able to remove the word from our heart. It becomes an invitation lost.

In Jesus' parable the seed needs to fall on good soil to grow and produce a crop. In the previous chapter we learned that in order to combat the enemy we needed to regularly pray, fast, and commit to praise and worship. Prayer, fasting, and praise and worship also prepare "good soil". These acts allow us to not only receive the word of God but to retain it, put it into practice, and flourish from it. It allows us to receive the invitation to dance, accept it, and never lose it to the enemy.

An Invitation Rejected

The hardest part of being smudged by the cinders is that we often feel there is no one we can trust with what is going on inside of us. Previous experiences have taught us that vulnerability opens us up to hurt and unfortunately we allow this distrust to carry over to our relationship with The Prince. This distrust causes us to reject the invitation to dance, reducing our Prince to a casual acquaintance. We don't have ready access to His thoughts and we have to guess at what God desires for us. We wind up wandering around lost and lonely.

Ella thought it impossible she could go to the ball in her current state. For a moment she had a glimmer of hope that maybe it was possible for someone like her to attend the ball and be seen as desirable by The Prince, however in the end she let doubt cloud her mind as she stared at her cinder smudge face in the mirror. In Ezra 9:6 the author laments, "O my God, I am too ashamed and disgraced to lift up my face to you, my God, because our sins are higher than our heads and our guilt has reached to the heavens." Guilt, sin, and shame will keep us from approaching God. It all goes back to those public sins, private sins, hurt, and emotional distress.

We often feel a need to change before we draw closer to our Savior. This actually begins a vicious cycle. We try to change ourselves to become worthy of His love and redemption but we fail because we are imperfect humans in need of a Savior to change the person we currently are. The impossibility of the task discourages us and we lose hope of ever being acceptable to Christ. It is hard for some of us to understand it takes supernatural divine power to be "perfect" and acceptable to Christ.

We are promised in 2 Corinthian 5:17 that if any man be in Christ, he is a new creation; the old is gone, the new has come! Transformation can not take place until after we've accepted the invitation. Old things are forgotten only when we are in Christ. Romans 8:37-39 says, "No, in all these things we are more than conquerors through him who loved us. For I am convinced that neither death nor life, neither angels nor demons, neither the present nor the future, nor any powers, neither height nor depth, nor anything else in all creation, will be able to separate us from the love of God that is in Christ Jesus our Lord." Once we realize who we are in Christ, we can not be separated from His love. We are more than conquerors thru Him that loved us. We are conquerors of our past and our present.

Pray Today:

Father,

I thank you for Your Messenger, the Holy Spirit. You send him to whoever will ask you for the gift of your Messenger. (Luke 11:13) I ask for his arrival today because it's through him I receive your invitation to dance. Today, I will not only accept the invitation to draw nearer to My Prince, Jesus as he draws near to me. (James 4:8) I refuse to allow the enemy to remove this invitation from my heart. Forgive me for ever rejecting the invitation. I realize now that you want me as I am and not the "perfect" person I tried to create in my own power. If I confess the cinders of my life to you, you are faithful and just to cleanse me of them. (1 John 1:9)

In the Name of Prince Jesus I Pray,

Amen

Magic Pumpkins and Glass Slippers

T he eve of the ball, Ella tearfully helped The Sisters and Duchess prepare. She mended hems, cut lace, and strung pearls. She trimmed split ends, plastered curls, and fastened ribbons. After what seemed an eternity Portia, Delilah, and Duchess were ready. In a whirlwind of sickening fragrance and tacky bustles they were gone. Ella looked around the empty house in despair. Overwhelmed, she ran out of the house to the orchard and wept bitterly.

"Why are you crying?" whispered a voice from the shadows of the many fruit trees. Startled Ella looked around her to see a gentle old woman sitting on a bench under a nearby apple tree. Smiling, the old woman made her way to the weeping girl. Kneeling next to Ella, the woman repeated, "Why are you crying?"

"Every one is going to the ball to see the Prince, but I can't go . . ."

"Because of your appearance?" the old women questioned.

"Isn't it horrible? Even if Duchess had said I could go, I couldn't meet The Prince like this. He would take one look at me and turn away from me," Ella sobbed.

"I agree; one can't meet The Prince in your state." The old woman stood up and began to pace. Ella watched her with curiosity. The old woman began to move about, humming and gesturing with her hands. Soon, Ella began to notice things dancing around her. First the largest pumpkin in the tiny patch she'd planted, then tiny mice that had just scurried out from under the pumpkin. Even their old blood hound Charlie seemed to prance about. Then in a burst of sparks, the pumpkin, the mice, and Charlie were gone. In their place stood a splendid diamond laced carriage tethered to four velvet black horses, and attended by a droopy eyed coachman.

"Oh my," Ella gasped, "How did you do that?"

The little woman chuckled, "Never you mind. Now we must do something about you. Hmmm, turn around, dear."

Ella began to turn. She turned and turned as the woman hummed and swayed. Ella began to feel dizzy but she continued to turn about because she had a feeling the old woman did not want her to stop. Finally, she fell to the soft ground, breathing heavily, asking, "Is that enough?"

"Of course. Look."

Ella looked down and realized she was wearing the most beautiful pale pink ball gown she had ever seen. It was even more beautiful than Portia and Delilah's expensive dresses imported from lands far away. Slowly, she stood trying to see every inch of the enchanted dress. As she spun she noticed a twinkling near the hem; it was her shoes! On her feet was dainty glass slippers sprinkled with diamonds.

"How can I thank you," Ella exclaimed with tears in her eyes.

"Just have fun. Go charm your Prince. You look the part of a princess now."

Ella's carriage was half way down the dirt path leading away from the Duchess' home when she heard the old woman yell behind her, "The magic ends at midnight. Remember, you only have until midnight!" Ella waved at the tiny crone. Midnight would give her more than enough time.

*   *   *

Moments later at the palace, a hush came over the main ballroom as Ella made it to the top of the ivory stairway. All eyes turned toward the astonishing princess floating down the stairs. Ella felt giddy as she curtsied finally reaching the bottom. Rising slowly she realized someone was standing before her with his hand out. It was The Prince!

"I've been waiting for you," He laughed.

"I've been waiting to meet you," Ella announced . . . a little too loudly. Out of the corner of her eye she was observing who could see her exchange with The Prince. A slight frown creased The Prince's face as he led Ella to the dance floor.

Ella was very aware of the effect her dress had on the crowd. She heard hushed whispers from all around. She made another deep curtsy before The Prince began twirling her around the floor. The night was turning out better than she could ever have imagined. As the Prince moved her expertly across the room, she caught sight of the Sisters turning a sickly shade of green, realizing someone besides them had caught the Prince's attention. She was beautiful and in front of the whole kingdom The Prince was falling in love with her.

"Why did you accept my invitation," The Prince asked.

Ella looked at the Prince quizzically. What an odd question. Who in their right mind wouldn't accept the invitation of the Prince? Before she could answer, Ella became distracted by the continued whispers from the crowd around her. They were in awe of her. Surely The Prince must love her even more now. The rest of the evening went by in a blur of music, dancing, and the kingdoms undivided attention on Ella. She barely heard a word The Prince said to her all evening. In her excitement, Ella forgot to watch the clock.

"Ella . . ."

"Yes, Prince," Ella sighed.

"You don't have to pretend for me," The Prince whispered.

Startled, she took a step back. Ella was prepared to deny pretending to be anything but the princess in front of him when it happened. The clock began to chime midnight. She watched as tiny splotches of cinder smudges began to pop up on her hand. The hem of her dress began to tater. Her hands flew to her face; she spun on her heels, and was soon flying up the ivory stairway.

"Ella!" The Prince bellowed after her but she was afraid to stop. Outside the carriage had already turned back into a pumpkin, the horses into mice, and there was good ole Charlie scratching a flea behind his ear. Ella ran faster and faster until she made it back home. When she was safely inside the house, she flung herself at her hearth and cried bitter tears. How could she have been so foolish? She'd forgotten to watch the clock. She'd become lost in the magic and for a moment she believed she was who she was pretending to be. A princess.

Chapter 7

When the Clock Strikes Twelve

Imagine you are Ella weeping bitterly in the garden as distant sounds from the ball filter through your ears. You are desperate to meet the Prince, but approaching Him in your current state is unfathomable. Then, out of nowhere, your Fairy Godmother arrives and turns everything around. All of sudden the cinders are gone, you are wearing a beautiful gown, and the whole world seems to dance around you. Now you are ready for the Prince. As you ride off into the moonlight, you vaguely remember the Fairy Godmother saying some nonsense about the clock striking midnight.

Be very wary of any solution that fixes things all of a sudden because it is usually too good to be true. Even the blessings of God don't come all of a sudden; when His blessings arrive, He has been working in the background preparing you and molding you to be ready for the blessing. All of a sudden fixes are usually temporary at best.

Temporary Magic

The Fairy Godmother's magic was temporary and superficial. Right under the surface remained all of Ella's problems and insecurities covered up by a pretty dress. Sooner than hoped for, Ella would turn back into the same little cinder girl. The Fairy Godmother is representative of man and religion. In our effort to have our cinders washed away, we often turn to religion to make us acceptable to man, hoping in the end it will make us acceptable to the Prince. Unfortunately the power of religion is temporary and lacks depth. Even if the cinders appear to have been washed away by religious ritual, they still lay there beneath the surface waiting for "the clock to strike twelve" to resurface stronger than ever.

I must take a moment now to define religion so that there is no confusion. When I say religion, I am not talking about church in general or the acceptance of Christ. Hebrews 10:25 says, "Let us not give up meeting together, as some are in the habit of doing, but let us encourage one another—and all the more as you see the Day approaching," and Romans 10:9 says, "That if you confess with your mouth, 'Jesus is Lord.' And believe in your heart God raised Him from the dead, you will be saved." I believe in the necessity of attending church on a regular basis and this book would be ridiculously unnecessary if I didn't believe in the redemptive qualities and saving grace of Jesus Christ. When I mention religion, I am talking about the legalistic mindset that can pop up when anyone focuses too much on doctrine and decorum (man's rules) rather than the saving grace of our Prince, Jesus. The Word of God has many commandments regarding how we are to govern ourselves but religiousness will lead one to believe that just our "acts" make us acceptable to Christ.

White Washed Tombs

Any time we hear about people leaning on their "good works" to ensure their salvation, most think about the Pharisees. In Matthew 23:27, Jesus confronts the local Pharisees about his feelings regarding their super holy shtick. He says, "You are like whitewashed tombs, which look beautiful on the outside but on the inside are full of dead men's bones and everything unclean." The Pharisees spent a lot of time spouting the law and making a show of being over the top holy. However, on the inside they stunk of death and unclean things. They thought their *acts* would make them deserving of God's unfailing love. They also assumed their outward *appearance* would prove to man how very righteous they were. They based they're entire being on the *approval* of man.

The interesting thing about the Pharisees is that all their pretending and posturing accomplished the opposite of what they intended. Their words and their actions were supposed to prepare them and make them deserving of the soon coming Messiah, yet in the end, they totally missed Him. Jesus had been in their midst, giving them an open invitation to the kingdom of heaven, but they missed it because they couldn't wrap their minds around a Savior who could love *a sinner* of all people.

I've read the Gospels more times than I can count. Yet, in all my readings, I don't think I ever identified with the Pharisees. When I came to verses about them, I wondered how a group of people could be so dense. How could anyone be so caught up in being the perfect picture of righteousness and holiness that they fail to see Jesus? I thought that if I were in their shoes I would have dropped the act and spent all my time getting to know the Son of God. It wasn't until I started writing this book that I realized that for many years I had pretty much lived the life of a Pharisee.

The Pharisees' main problem wasn't their hypocrisy (although that was very bad); it was their inability to trust God with their whole heart. God knows us inside and out. It's foolish to think we can hide what is in our hearts, however, a few years back I attempted to do exactly that. Instead of just trusting the Father with my heart and who I really was, I focused on acts, appearance, and approval to become worthy of the Prince.

Acts

As I struggled with my own cinders and my own feelings of unworthiness, I found myself working in the youth ministry. From the very beginning, I loved being a part of the youth leadership team, however, a lot of my self-worth as a leader hinged on the praise of the youth pastor. I would work tirelessly developing new programs, planning activities, and teaching. Unfortunately, none of my work really had anything to do with the spiritual development of the young minds God had entrusted to me. Did I want them saved? Yes. Did I want them to live holy and pure lives? Absolutely! Yet my main focus was what else I could do to have my "faith" validated by our leader. I wrongly thought that if I worked hard enough and others saw it, then I would be worthy to the Prince.

What we have to realize is that it is not our good "acts" that make us worthy of the Prince. Ephesians 2:8, 9 explains, "For it is by grace you have been saved, through faith—and this not from yourselves, it is the gift of God—*not by works*, so that no one can boast." (NLT, emphasis mine.) We should all work hard and diligently in our ministry but it is important that we regularly evaluate the reason behind our hard work. When it stops being about the furtherance of the kingdom and becomes about man's praise, we need to take a step back and refocus our energies on growing closer to our Prince. It is by His grace we have been saved and our cinders are washed away. It had nothing to do with anything we have done. Our past acts cannot make Christ love us any less just as numerous acts for the approval of man cannot make Him love us anymore.

Approval

Many Cinder Girls suffer from approval addiction. We will turn ourselves upside down to make sure that we receive approval from those around us. Sometimes we compromise who we are just to receive the feeling that we are accepted and approved by a group. I know a young woman who finds it difficult to fit in with the other people her age at church. When she is around them, she feels awkward and out of place. She told me once that she could see it in their eyes that they believed she was just as out of place. For many years she tried to change her behavior and her interests so that she could find their approval in order to fit into their group. But each attempt to gain their approval of who she'd tried to become was met with more awkwardness. Her desperate need to fit in came from a fear of being alone. She wanted friends who had the same beliefs as she did but if she did not fit in with the people in her ministry and she could no longer comfortably spend time with the unbelievers she knew, where did that leave her?

Fear usually drives us to attain approval in ways we should not. It took the young woman several years to realize she was trying to fit in where God would never allow her to be comfortable. The other young people in the ministry were saved and passionate about Christ, however the calling and anointing God had placed on her was unique and unusual. In order to fully receive true approval from the group she would have to bury that anointing. When she began to understand that concept she was able to seek approval from the correct source, Our King. Sometimes it meant being lonely but understanding she was never alone. She began wanting to please God more than man and she found peace in her heart. 2 Chronicles16:9 says that the eyes of the Lord range throughout the earth to strengthen those whose hearts are fully committed to him. If we are totally committed to pleasing him, he strengthens our hearts so that we hunger less for man's approval.

There is nothing wrong with wanting to be a part of a group or to desire companionship; God created us as sociable creatures. However, we must be careful not to change the person God called us to be in order to "fit in". Approval from man does not then make us approved by God.

Appearance

One of my favorite songs has always been Charlie Chaplin's "Smile". I recently just began to meditate on the words of the song and it surprised me how bad the advice is in it. "Smile, though your heart is aching.

Smile, even though it's breaking. When there are clouds in the sky, you'll get by." What a beautiful melody with slightly warped advice. We've all heard "Fake it til you make it". That's really what the song is saying. Smile until everything is worth smiling about. Don't let them see you sweat.

The problem for most Cinder Girls is that we have made this our personal mantra. Don't let anyone close enough to see what's inside or you may be rejected. Keep the smile on, say "I'm having a blessed day", hug your neighbor, and whatever you do don't let the world know it's all a fragile mask that could break at any moment. We don't feel so worthy and holy on the inside but if we *appear* super holy on the outside, eventually it will all match, right? The issue becomes we don't only try to pull this magic act with man but fairly soon we try to pull it with God. "Look God, I look really holy and religious. I'll eventually get it right on the inside. Am I worthy of your Prince, now?" I'm sorry to say that is not how it works.

Sometimes we have to wear our heart on our sleeves. I know it is so hard, but it is important that when we come before our Prince, we are transparent. He isn't looking for pretenders. He isn't seeking someone who appears to be committed to Him, but someone who truly *is* committed to him. We don't have to pretend with Jesus. On those days where you feel like every move you make is wrong, tell Jesus. When you feel perfectly flawed, tell Jesus. When you are struggling with your past, tell Jesus. None of it comes as a surprise to him. He's not looking for perfection or piousness. Psalms 51:6 says, "Surely you desire truth in the inner parts; you teach me wisdom in the inmost place." We don't have to *appear* to be anything we are not. God is looking for someone who will be honest and in our openness is where he will teach us wisdom to handle the struggles in life.

Pray Today:

Father,

I thank you for the grace and mercy that can only be found in Prince Jesus. Your word reminds me that there is now no condemnation for those who are in Christ Jesus. (Romans 8:1) I don't have to worry about the approval of man because even if my mother and father forsake me, You, Lord, will receive me. (Psalm 27:10) I know that it is not by my acts or the appearance of holiness that makes me acceptable to You, but I am made acceptable by your grace. (Ephesians 2:8-9)

In the Name of Prince Jesus I Pray,

Amen

The Prince's Pursuit

"**Y**our Highness?"

The Prince turned from His balcony which provided Him a view of the entire kingdom to find The Messenger beside Him. "My Princess, she is still with the Duchess?"

"Yes, sire." The Messenger answered.

"And the cinders?"

"Her face is still smudged by them."

The Prince looked back over His kingdom sadly. Ella still didn't realize who she was to Him. He'd chased after her as she rushed away from the ball but she'd run away too quickly. Just then, The King entered. He had been watching Ella all along. When the dark forces had taken her, they'd cast a spell that could only be broken when Ella claimed her authority as Princess of his kingdom, but she had not done so yet. It broke his heart to see The Princess being held captive by The Duchess. He drummed his fingers on the marble railing of the balcony, and then turned to The Prince and The Messenger resolute.

"Go get her," he ordered.

"Sire?" The Messenger questioned.

"Go claim our Princess! Do whatever it takes!"

"Yes, sire," The Prince responded excitedly.

"Immediately, great King," The Messenger added.

"Prepare her for my arrival," The Prince yelled over his shoulder at The Messenger as He gathered his sword and shield, "and watch out for The Duchess. She will not let Ella go without a fight."

In almost an instant The Messenger arrived at the home of The Duchess. With great authority he pounded on the large oak door at the front of the home. His head buzzed with anticipation. Finally The

Princess would be free. She had been through a very grueling journey but it had prepared her for this moment. When Ella opened the door, he smiled widely.

"Your highness," he exclaimed as he bowed deeply.

"I'm sorry?" Ella answered with a confused uncertain smile.

"I have come to inform you that . . ."

"Ella, go to your room!" The Messenger and Ella watched as The Duchess barreled down the long hallway towards them.

"Yes, Duchess," Ella replied and scurried away.

"Who are you," The Duchess barked at the man standing at her front door.

"I am The Messenger for The Crown Prince of this land and you should not have sent the child away." The Messenger eyed The Duchess warily with his hand on the hilt of his own sword.

"You are not welcomed here."

"I am welcomed anywhere The Prince sends me and he has sent me to this place to prepare for his arrival."

"So The Prince is on his way here," The Duchess questioned, "Well, let him come. I am ready for him."

"He is ready for you," The messenger countered as the sound of hooves could be heard galloping up the walk way. Without hesitation, The Prince swung off his saddle and marched past The Messenger and The Duchess into the house. He glanced about him and wondered how Ella could have dwelled in such misery for so long.

"I did not invite you in," The Duchess seethed.

Ignoring The Duchess completely, he searched for a sign of Ella. At that moment, Portia and Delilah entered the room. Quickly the sisters flanked The Prince as The Duchess pushed The Messenger outside, locked the door, and took position behind The Prince. He caught the movement from his peripheral but remained unconcerned. Where was Ella? The Duchess and the sisters were prepared to attack when they all heard footsteps on the main stairway.

"I'm sorry Duchess, but I forgot my duster," Ella called down the stairs, finally coming into view.

"Ella," The Prince sighed

CHAPTER 8

The Prince

The hero of any true fairytale, be it Cinderella or Snow White, is the prince. He is the one who emerges victorious from every obstacle that lies between him and his beloved princess. His sword shines brightly, blazing mightily through the hearts of his enemies. He is strong, just, courageous, and the most handsome in all the land. The fairytale prince is all this, yet, he is still but a pale imitation of the One True Prince. When all is said and done there isn't an imagined hero who can stand up against our Savior, Jesus.

The Character of The Prince

The character of our Prince should be an easy section to write but each time I sat down to type I came down with an insane case of writer's block. I had intended on using another of my favorite passages of scripture, Psalms 45, to describe the character of Jesus. It is a great passage and probably would have been adequate however I didn't have peace about using the passage. At one point I had decided to just Google what others had said about the character of Jesus but I didn't even get a new browser window open before I heard, "Who do you say I am?"

Peter is often the disciple I identify with most. Ninety-five percent of the time he was going to put his foot in his mouth. He had poor impulse control, he was passionate to a fault, he had his bossy moments, and when the chips were down he regrettably denied Christ. That is me to the umpteenth degree. However, Jesus still trusted him to build his church here on earth. Why? I believe it has something to do with an incident that occurred in Matthew 16.

Jesus and his disciples arrived in the villages of Caesera Philipi. Completely unexpected, Jesus asks, "What are the people saying about who the Son of Man is?" I can imagine the disciples stumbling over there words, trying to give what they believed was the appropriate answer. Their answers ranged from John the Baptizer, Elijah, Jeremiah, to one of the other prophets. Jesus pressed them, "Who do *you* say that I am?" In all his impulsive glory, Peter declares, "You're Christ, the Messiah, the Son of the living God." It was that simple for Peter. He had been traveling with Jesus for quite some time now; there was no doubt in Peter's mind who stood before him. Jesus praised Peter because this wasn't knowledge Peter had gleaned from a book or other scholars. Jesus's response was, "God bless you, Simon, son of Jonah! You didn't get that answer out of books or from teachers. My Father in heaven, God himself, let you in on this secret of who I really am. And now I'm going to tell you who you are, really are. You are Peter, a rock. This is the rock on which I will put together my church, a church so expansive with energy that not even the gates of hell will be able to keep it out."

Peter's knowledge of who Christ was came directly from the heart of our Father, God. When questioned about Jesus's identity, Peter responded with what he had learned by spending time with Jesus and what God had shown him. I now have that question before me; who do I say he is? What have I learned about Jesus by drawing near to him?

He is a warrior who will conquer our enemy with just the words that proceed from his mouth. (Revelation 19:11-15) He is bold in the face of injustice and sin. (Matthew 21:12) He is a healer when my heart is broken. (Psalm 34:18) He is jealous for me. (Exodus 20:5) He is confident in the face of temptation. (Luke 4) He is gracious and merciful to the point of being sacrificed on the cross for my sins. (John 3:16) He is a courageous Prince who rides for truth, humility, and righteousness. (Psalm 45:4. Okay so I got part of it in here.) He is holy which mean he is set-apart from the things of this world. (Psalm 22:3) He is the author and finisher of both my faith and my love story. (Hebrews 12:2) I can go on. During my journey out of the cinders learning who Jesus was in my life was not optional. When you begin to develop a relationship with someone, you take a look at the person's character. Who they are and what they believe are important. Most of us wouldn't knowingly enter an intimate relationship with a murderous liar. We wouldn't feel truly comfortable in their presence and would always have our guard up.

If you are to ever live a cinder free existence, you will need a true no holds bar relationship with our Prince. You will have to trust him completely in order to surrender to him and have faith in how he feels about you. However, if you know nothing about who he is, how can you possibly trust him? How can you love him? I can spend all day telling about who he is to me. I can expound on the characteristics I find awe-inspiring in Jesus and the images of him that make me want to cry tears of joy but it will do nothing for you if you do not discover these things for yourself. As you continue on this journey out of the cinders, take time to learn about The Prince who calls you to a cinder free life with him.

The Desire of The Prince

Jesus desires a romance with us. He desires an intimate relationship with us. Everything He has done is to draw us closer to our King and to him, our Prince. Just like a new groom rejoices over his bride, God rejoices over us. (Isaiah 62:5) Matthew 25 describes Jesus as a bridegroom coming for his bride, the church. It depicts the need to be ready because we never know when our bridegroom will return for us. In John 3:29 Jesus makes reference to himself as the bridegroom. Throughout scripture we find that our Savior isn't looking for a casual acquaintance, he is seeking a true relationship with each one of us.

This is why throughout God's word our relationship with our Prince is compared to a courtship, a wedding, and a marriage.

The desire of The Prince is that we know him intimately and accept him as our headship. He wants to protect us and care for us as would an earthly husband for his wife. Ephesians 5:25-27 says, "Husbands love your wives, just as Christ loved the church and gave himself up for her to make her holy, cleansing her by washing with water through the word, and to present her to himself as a radiant church, without stain or wrinkle or any other blemish, but holy and blameless." How breathtaking is that? Our Prince sacrificed himself on the cross in order that we could be set-apart and cleansed of our cinders through the word so that we can stand before him a radiant bride without stain, wrinkle, or blemish from our past. He conquered death because he desired to draw us nearer as his holy and blameless bride.

Sometimes it is difficult to believe that such an awesome God could desire anything from us. It is hard to understand how he could want cinder smudged us to stand next to him as his beautiful princess, but the Bible screams out that this is exactly what our Prince longs for. It is what God, our King desires. He sent his Son to die for us so that we could have an abundant life as his royal daughters. (John 10:10)

The Pursuit of The Prince

Some of us are old enough to remember the old Looney Toons' character, Pepe Le Pew. Pepe was a skunk that didn't know he smelled. Every episode, somehow, a black female cat would accidentally have a white stripe painted down her back and would then cross Pepe's path. Pepe, assuming it was a female skunk would immediately fall in love and pursue her with almost laughable tenacity. She would hide and he would inevitably find her. She would run and he would calmly trot after her. He was never in a hurry, never worried that he would not catch her, and never once did it concern him that she was running from him. There will be people in my yard with torches and pitchforks after they read this statement but Jesus's pursuit of us is much like Pepe the cartoon skunk.

Our Prince isn't in a hurry. It doesn't worry him if we try to hide from him or pull away from him. He pursues us doggedly and it doesn't cross his mind that he won't catch us. His only concern is how long will we allow ourselves to dwell in a cindered existence before we turn around and fall into the arms of The Prince that is chasing after us.

The Chase

Bob Dylan wrote a song many years ago called, "To Make You Feel My Love". It's a simple but very poignant song about the lengths he would go to make his significant other know how much he loves her. One verse goes:

When the rain is blowing in your face
And the whole world is on your case
I could offer you a warm embrace
To make you feel my love

Hosea 2:14-15 happens to be one of my favorite passages of scripture. It always reminds me that the Bible is really a very large anthology of love letters from our God to us. Bob Dylan's song mirrors what God is saying in these verses. In this passage it says, "And now, here's what I'm going to do: I'm going to start all over again. I'm taking her back out into the wilderness where we had our first date, and I'll court her. I'll give her bouquets of roses. I'll turn Heartbreak Valley into Acres of Hope. She'll respond like she did as a young girl, those days when she was fresh out of Egypt." (The Message) God is a righteous, holy, and revered deity. He deserves to be feared and worshiped, yet more than anything He wishes for us to love Him and for us to know His love. He is willing to go back to square one, move heaven and earth, sacrifice His only Son just to make us aware of His feelings toward us. That is the dogged tenacity with which our King and our Prince chase after us.

Can you imagine Him singing the above lyrics to you? *My daughter, when the rains of life are blowing in your face and the world is on your case, My princess, I offer you a warm embrace so that you can feel My love for you.* God meets us in our desert experiences (cinder smudged existence) and speaks words of comfort to bring us closer to Him. He shows us our situation is only a stopping station on our journey to who we really are in Him. The God of the universe wants to be loved by you. The Savior of all mankind knows everything about you and still sees the royal daughter of The King whom he adores. Meditate on those statements for a moment. It's a heady thought, isn't it? If God would chase us down to give us his heart, what does he request in return? He asks only for our heart back. If we give ourselves over fully to him, have faith in him, and believe in him everything else will fall in place. This is not to say there will never be difficult times but I would rather go through a stormy situation in the embrace of our Prince than alone in a bed of cinders. How about you?

Pray Today:

Father,

I thank you for desiring me to draw closer to you and for pursuing me with such energy. I want to learn more about who The Prince is in my life. When I draw closer to you, you draw closer to me. (James 4:8) Father, open the eyes of my heart so that I may truly see Jesus and be blessed. (Matthew 13:16) My eyes and my heart will always be focused on you. (Psalm 25:15)

In the Name of Prince Jesus I Pray,

Amen

The Beautiful Princess Revealed

At the sight of The Prince standing in the hallway, tears of relief and pain began to seep from Ella's eyes. She fell desperate at His feet and wept bitterly. Everything she had endured rushed back to her; all of her foolishness, all of her shame, and all her hurt. Ella cried for the life she had been leading, but none of it mattered. The Prince was here and even if He was here to throw her into the dungeon for impersonating a princess, she took a small comfort in the fact that wherever The Prince took her was better than her current situation.

"Please . . . ," Ella begged.

"Ella, get up right now! You are not to touch The Prince"

"Mother, leave her be. What could poor, dirty, Cinder Ella, possibly do to The Prince" Portia sneered.

"Portia is right, Mother," Delilah cackled, "She is only embarrassing herself in front of The Prince."

"Girls, be quiet! Ella! Leave this instant! I will not have you embarrass me in front of The Prince."

The Prince knelt down to touch Ella's hand. Ella slowly looked up to see The Prince's kind face covered in concern. Tears brimmed in His eyes. In His eyes she saw her own pain reflected. Before she could speak, The Duchess grabbed her arm painfully, trying to snatch Ella away from The Prince. Ella again met The Prince's eyes finding in them an indignation that seemed to course through her veins. Ella for a moment found a strength she'd never known before. Wrenching her arm free from The Duchess, she ran back towards The Prince.

"This is me, cinder smudges and all. I'm just a kitchen girl. The dress, the hair, the shoes . . . all of it was a fake. I'm a fake. I'm not the beautiful princess you danced with at the ball," Ella let the words fall from her lips.

The Duchess's face turned bright red as she yelled, "Ella, I command you to leave the room this instance."

Ella took another step towards The Prince. "I'm not a princess . . ."

"Ella, leave NOW!"

Ella spun to face The Duchess. "Be quiet! Just . . . be quiet! I have listened to you all my life. You have told me how unworthy of love I am. You have told me how ugly I am. But my father, he used to call me beautiful and treasured. I know that today I am a kitchen maid. I know where I've come from and where I am now, but I promise you this; no matter what happens today, you . . . no . . . longer . . . control me!" Ella seethed.

The Duchess's face contorted in anger. Slowly her skin began to turn a shimmery shade of emerald green. Scales formed on her hands and face. Ella watched in horror as The Duchess's form faded into that of an enormous slithering serpent. Ella tried to flee but she found herself held in place by two rancid trolls who were hissing and spitting at her. It was Portia and Delilah!

"You are mine. I own you," the serpent hissed.

"Evil One!"

The serpent's head swiveled at the sound of The Prince's voice and warily eyed The Prince's drawn sword. "I believe Ella commanded you to be silent. I now command you to leave."

"Death first," The Evil One hissed.

"So be it," The Prince stated as he moved confidently toward the large serpent. The Evil One and The Prince circled one another only once before they charged. The battle was over quickly. The Prince was too quick and too powerful for The Evil One. A skilled swing of His sword and The Evil One fell to the ground defeated. The trolls that had seized Ella fell just as fast as His sword arced through the air, expertly finding its intended targets.

Ella stared stunned. She watched as The Prince sheathed His weapon and approached.

"What just happened?" Ella exclaimed.

"Ella, do you remember what your father used to call you?"

"Yes. My father used to call me 'The Beautiful Princess'."

"It wasn't just a nickname. You truly are a princess. The Duchess was really The Evil One and it was her goal to make sure you would never remember that you are beyond a shadow of a doubt . . ." The Prince started.

"The Beautiful Princess?"

"Yes. I've been waiting for you. I've come to rescue you. I just needed you to silence the voice of The Evil One."

"You are wrong!"

"Ella . . ." The Prince started.

"No," Ella interrupted. She took a deep breath and continued, "Let me finish what I have to say. You just think I'm The Beautiful Princess but I am not. I know I don't deserve someone as magnificent as you but I love you. I promise that, if you could just love me in return, my whole heart is yours for eternity. I won't hide a single part of myself from you. You have everything and I have nothing. You are courageous and I am fearful. You are strong and I am weak. I may never be that girl you met at the ball but maybe . . . just maybe . . . you could love me as a poor cinder-smudged kitchen girl as much as you loved me when You thought I was a brilliant princess."

Ella stared at her feet and waited for his response for what seemed like forever. When The Prince's laugh began to echo through the room, poor Ella's heart began to break. He was laughing at her! Ella turned to leave but his hand reached out to stop her. All of a sudden she was looking into the powerful, loving eyes of The Prince.

"Ella, this is what I've been trying to tell you," he chuckled. The Prince raised his hand and gently touched her soot stained cheek. "I do love you. I've always known who you were and to me you have always been beautiful. You believe you aren't the princess from the night of the ball. You keep telling me it was all a façade and you are partly right. You aren't the princess from the ball . . . you are oh so much more! What you were pretending to be pales in comparison to who you really are. You are the Beautiful Princess. You just can't see it, but I can!"

With that, he pulled a slender gold crown laced with diamonds rubies and emeralds from his pocket and placed it on her head. "My delight is in you, Ella. It is you I want to marry. What else can I do to prove I love you? I will go to the very ends of the Earth and fight the most ferocious dragon. I will do it if in the end you truly understand the depths of my love for you," The Prince held her chin and looked intently into her eyes," Do you trust Me, Ella?"

"Yes . . ." she whispered.

"Do you trust Me to love you even knowing that you have spent your life as a simple cinder girl?"

"Yes," Ella answered with more confidence.

"Finally, do you trust My love with your whole heart? Will you give your heart over to Me and trust Me to never take My love away?"

"I do," she spoke with finality

"Most importantly Ella, do you love Me?"

"More than I've ever loved myself, Prince!"

When he was certain she meant it, he walked her slowly to the mirror in the hall and stood her before it. Ella gasped. Staring back at her was the most Beautiful Princess she had ever seen. This Princess was lovelier than the Fairy Godmother could have ever made her! The woman in the mirror had a stunning gown woven with gold thread on. At her neck, there was a small string of pearls and her smile was almost blinding. Her very countenance was brilliant and extravagant. Tears were running down the woman's face. Ella turned towards The Prince.

"That cannot be me."

"It is you," The Prince smiled.

"But . . . how?"

"You just had to see yourself the way I've always seen you. You could only do that if you truly trusted me with your whole heart. You have been and forever will be My Princess and My Bride."

"And you will always be My Prince and My Husband."

Years passed by and from time to time Princess Ella would cross the path of someone who wondered, "Aren't you that cinder girl from the village below?" Princess Ella would smile brightly, feel the presence of her Prince beside her, and reply "Yes . . . once upon a time I was she, but no longer." And as you can imagine, she and her Prince lived happily ever after . . .

 CHAPTER 9

Happily Ever After

You have sinned and been plagued with guilt. You've been hurt and suffered from despair. The King's love has felt far away and you didn't know where he was. Cinder Stokers have attacked you and Cinder Dwellers have almost caused you to doubt your royal position. You desired The Prince with all your heart but briefly put your faith in man to make you worthy of his love only to find yourself continually falling short. However, now, you have learned about whom your Prince is in your life, you've discovered the desires of his heart, and felt him pursue you. He has slain the enemy and freed you from your bondage. Happily ever after is within your grasp dear Princess, just a few more steps left in our journey.

Clearing Away The Baggage

Even after watching The Prince slay The Duchess, Ella still didn't see herself as a Princess. She believed The Prince had come all that way for a princess that had been conjured up by magic but hoped he would settle for a poor cinder girl who loved him terribly. Most of us have a hard time seeing ourselves the way Jesus sees us. We see the past. We see our sins. We see ourselves through the eyes of the world. So even after Jesus has pursued us so tenaciously, it is hard to believe he hasn't come to punish us. Jesus, The Prince, sees the bride he adores and loves. However, He realizes that no matter how He sees us, we will never have true intimacy with Him until He washes the cinders from our face and what He sees begins to match what we see. This takes some action on our part.

As hard as it might seem, we must confess everything that is in our heart; we must confess the good, the bad, and the ugly. We must place everything before Him; public sins, private sins, hurt, and our feelings must be laid bare before Him. 1 John 1:9 says, "If we confess our sins, he is faithful and just and will forgive us our sins and purify us from all unrighteousness. Then Psalm 32:5 reminds us that after we confess what is inside, not only are our sins forgiven, but the *guilt* of our sins is forgiven. We don't have to feel the guilt of our past anymore when we are completely honest with our Prince.

Jesus wants a relationship with us but as in any relationship before trust and intimacy can be obtained, old baggage must be cleared away. When Ella first confronted The Prince after He found her in Duchess's home, she confessed everything in her heart. She said, "This is me, cinder smudges and all. I'm just a kitchen girl. The dress, the hair, the shoes . . . all of it was a fake. I'm a fake. I'm not the beautiful princess you danced with at the ball . . . ." At some point we all need to have this conversation with Christ. We all need to say, "I can't save myself. Everything I am and everything I've tried to be is nothing compared to You. Can you love me, this me, anyway?" Amazingly, His answer is yes! Not only does he say yes, he proclaims we are so much more than just cinder girls. He whispers to us, "You are my princess."

The Journey Begins

Even with total confession, there are still steps we need to take before we can say we have fully left our cindered existence behind us. Each chapter in this book has been preparing us for this moment, the moment we begin our cinder free life. In any journey, we need a road map to understand how to reach our destination. The following steps are our road map. Everything that proceeded was in preparation to take this journey. Think of the previous chapters as us acquiring the equipment needed to travel. Jesus can wash away the cinders smudging our face, calling us his Beautiful Princess, but if we don't leave the cinders behind us, eventually our face will again become smudged. Now it is time to begin our journey out of the cinders forever.

Remember The Words of The King

Remember your word to your servant, for you have given me hope. My comfort in my suffering is this: Your promise preserves my life. The arrogant mock me without restraint, but I do not turn from your law. I remember *your ancient laws, O Lord, and I find comfort in them. ~Psalm 119:49-52*

Our journey out of the cinders begins with one very simple step; remember the words of our Father in heaven. Part of the reason many of us remain so long in a cindered existence is because we meditate on the wrong words and messages. We concentrate on what the world says about us. We focus on the message cinder stokers and dwellers recite to us daily; we begin to internalize it and the enemy uses it to keep us bound. It was at the moment Ella began to remember the words her father had spoken into her life that she began to truly combat her enemy.

Regular bible study is essential in a cinder girl's life. God's word tells us who we really are. The truth of the Father combats the lies of the devil. It's in the words of the Father we find the hope of Jesus our Prince, comfort during times of suffering, and a promise of life. Setting aside time every day to meditate on God's word will keep us focused on His love, acceptance, and His sovereignty. The more time you spend memorizing and internalizing His words, the less power the enemy will have to keep you in the ashes.

Realize You Can Not Wash Away Your Own Cinders

. . .   But you were washed, you were sanctified, you were justified in the name of the Lord Jesus Christ and by the Spirit of our God. ~1 Corinthians 6:11

We've said this many times throughout the book but it is important to remember. *We cannot wash away our pasts.* We don't have the power. The Power lies with our Prince Jesus and to forget this will find us again stuck in the cinders of life. Where we often fail in our attempt to live a cinder free existence is when we trust in our own power to wash the smudges away from our face. As mentioned before, we regularly depend on our acts, appearance, and the acceptance of others to cleanse us and make us a princess worthy of the Prince. Yet Titus 3:5 says, " . . . He saved us, not because of the righteous things we had done, but because of his mercy. He saved us through the washing rebirth and renewal by the Holy Spirit." At the instant you realize you cannot wash away your cinders and that cleansing comes from the power given to our Prince, you can begin living a cinder free existence.

Release Your Cinder Stokers

Bear with each other and forgive whatever grievances you may have against one another. Forgive as the Lord forgave you. ~Colossians 3:13

The hardest yet most crucial stop on our journey out of the cinders is forgiveness. It is necessary to forgive those who may have hurt you; release the anger. When someone hurts us, we want to hold on to that pain until they can feel it too, wondering why God has not punished them yet. However, releasing (forgiving) your cinder stoker is actually more about you than making them feel better.

Interestingly enough, in most cases, while you harbor anger and resentment for a cinder stoker, they have moved on and aren't aware that you are angry. Holding on to past grievances and hurts builds up within you; you are the only one affected by it. I recently read that anger shuts down the immune system for 6 hours. Imagine holding on to anger for years! What are you doing to yourself physically and emotionally when you can't release your cinder stoker?

In the end, releasing your cinder stoker is required by our heavenly Father. When we cannot release those who have sinned against us, we cannot be released from our own sins. If you want to live a cinder free existence, be aware you will have to take the big step and forgive those who may have helped you into the cinders in the first place. Note forgiveness is not a feeling, it is an act. We must actively forgive even when we do not feel like it. Daily we submit our anger and hurt to God, continuing to forgive until one morning; there is no more anger and pain.

Repent For All Distractions & Sins That Separated You From The Prince

Therefore, since we are surrounded by such a great cloud of witnesses, let us throw off everything that hinders and the din that do easily entangles, and let us run with perseverance the race marked out for us. Let us fix our eyes on Jesus, the author and finisher of our faith . . . ~Hebrews 12:1, 2

Repentance is a necessity in any Christian's walk with Christ. When you repent, you consciously turn from sin to God, sorry for what you've done previously, and resolving not to do it again. It takes a profound change of mind from sin-centeredness to God-centeredness. In our journey into the cinders we allowed various emotions, situations, and sins to separate us from the Prince. In order to move closer to Him, we must turn away from those distractions and turn to Jesus, the author and finisher of our faith. We ask for forgiveness and then we let go of our past mistakes, realizing that The Prince has let go of them as well.

Remove Cinder Dwellers From Your Life

"Therefore come out from them and be separate," says the Lord, "Touch no unclean thing and I will receive you."~2 Corinthians 6:17

We are commanded in the bible to not be yoked together with unbelievers. The question is posed, what does a believer have in common with an unbeliever? The more I study this passage of scripture, the more I am convinced that this doesn't refer to just those who are not members of the body of Christ. The Greek word translated as unbeliever in this passage means, "without faith". Cinder Dwellers may be in church day and night. They may believe in Christ but they do not have faith in who the Word of God says he is. While we should always encourage our brothers and sisters, our running buddy should not be a faithless person. They should not be our confidant because their advice would come from a place of little or no faith. When we are journeying out of the cinders, we need to surround ourselves with people who have faith coming out of their ears so they can help bolster our own faith. Iron sharpens iron.

Reject The Power Of The Enemy

They overcame him [Satan] by the blood of the Lamb and by the word of their testimony; they did not love their lives so much as to shrink from death. ~Revelations 12:11

Satan only has the power to keep you bound if you give it to him. As you begin to meditate on the Word of God, rely on Christ to cleanse you, forgive your cinder stokers, remove distractions, and separate yourself from cinder dwellers, you begin to loosen the grip of the enemy over your life. However, to overcome, the word says we need the blood of Jesus that washes away all sins and to testify. Holding in what Jesus has done for you may mean another woman may never know that she can live a cinder free life. Has this book blessed your heart at all? Imagine for a moment if I had decided not to testify about my journey out of the cinders. Think of the many women who would not have heard the message that they are Beautiful Princesses in the court of The King of Kings.

When we refuse to be ashamed of whom we once were we steal power away from the enemy. When we share with others what The Prince has done for us, it glorifies The Prince and diminishes the hold of Satan over other people's lives. It also reminds us of our Kings love for us. There is power in our words. Satan is aware of this which is why he tries to silence us when we begin to declare the truths of The Prince. However, just by sharing what you've been through removes the sting of his attacks. When you declare the works of Jesus regardless of what the enemy throws at you, his attempts become futile against you.

I also want to mention that it is necessary to pray for guidance as to what our King wants you to share. While true deliverance should always be shared, telling *every* detail is not always right or needed. Some parts of your testimony God may release you to tell everyone; in other instances he will lead you to tell only one person. Be prayerful and pay close attention to the leading of God through the Holy Spirit.

Rejoice and Dance With Your Prince

Oh, love me—and right now!—hold me tight! Just the way you promised. Now comfort me so I can live, really live; your revelation is the tune I dance to. ~Psalm 119:76, 77

Does happily ever after seem possible now? As you've discovered more about who you are and who The Prince is, does happily ever after now seem feasible? I pray happily ever after for you dear Princess. The Prince is waiting for you to take his hand and dance with him into the cinder free life he has prepared for you. He promises to hold on tightly and never let go. The revelation he gives when we draw near to him will be the tune you dance to. Psalm 119:73-77 says:

73 With your very own hands you formed me; now breathe your wisdom over me so I can understand you.

74 When they see me waiting, expecting your Word, those who fear you will take heart and be glad.

75 I can see now, God, that your decisions are right; your testing has taught me what's true and right.

76 Oh love me—and right now!—hold me tight! just the way you promised.

77 Now comfort me so I can live, really live; your revelation is the tune I dance to.

Rejoice in knowing you were formed by the hands of our King. He will breath into us understanding of the Triune God; Father, Son, and Holy Ghost. When people see you waiting and expecting God's promises, other Princesses will take heart and be glad because they know only a woman who understands her royal position in the Kingdom of God could wait so faithfully on the promises of God. Your cinder experience has taught you what is both true and right. Now bask in the love of your Prince. Feel his arms wrapped tightly and live, Princess.

Pray Today:

Father,

I thank you for washing the cinders from my face and making me new. (Psalm 51:7) I thank you for calling me Princess, bringing me out of a cindered existence, and making me glorious in your eyes. (Psalm 45:13) Continue to love me and hold me tight as you have promised. I will dance daily with The Prince and draw ever closer to him. (Psalm 149:3) I will forever praise you because I am no longer smudged by the cinders.

In the Name of Prince Jesus I Pray,

Amen